Basketball's Match-Up Defense

Every man who knows how to read has it in his power to magnify himself, to multiply the ways in which he exists, to make his life full, significant, and interesting.

—Aldous Huxley

Basketball's Match-Up Defense

CHARLES R. WARD

Head Basketball Coach
Nova High School
Ft. Lauderdale, Fla.

PRENTICE-HALL, INC., *Englewood Cliffs, N.J.*

PRINTED IN THE UNITED STATES OF AMERICA

07245–BC

TO MY DAUGHTER LYNDA
AND TO MY SON MARK

Acknowledgments

It is hoped that the material in this manuscript will be used by coaches to develop future defensive theory that is beyond the realm of offensive theory. The text has been satisfying because an opportunity is made available to expand ideas of the late Cam Henderson who originated the zone defense and the fast break.

My thanks to Garland Pinholster for introducing the material to Prentice-Hall, Inc.

Special thanks must go to Herb Karl, my assistant at Nova High School, for his critique of the material, for his grammatical help, and for his formulation of the scouting material.

I want to thank Miss Margaret Paysinger for grammatical help during the early stages of the text, Robert Bates for help with the art work, and Mrs. Evelyn F. Dugan, typist.

CHARLIE WARD

7

CONTENTS

1. THE MATCH-UP   **14**

What is the Match-Up?   **15**
*Combines strong points of all defenses. Defensive
front changes constantly.*

What Are the Advantages of the Match-Up?   **22**
*Effective against individual strengths and weaknesses.
Effective against a driving, screening type of defense.
Troublesome to the outside shooter. Effective for us
of big slow men. Effective when you are in foul trouble.
Excellent for defensive rebounding. Advantageous
for fast breaking. Effective against regular defense.
Effective on any size court.*

2. BASIC DRILLS FOR TEACHING THE MATCH-UP   **38**
The Position Master   **40**

Defensive Stance   **41**
*Check defensive posture. Placement of the feet.
Role of the toes and knees. Use of the arms and hands.*

Defensive Implications   46
Position hints. Mental hints. Observation hints.

Footwork and Shifting Drills   49
*Directional slide and shift drill. Start and stop drill.
Shift-slide-pass drill. Rubber ball drill. Dribble get-
back-on-defense drill. One-two-three drill. Three-on-
three full-court. Short-cut drill. Three-on-three with
a screen drill. Three-on-three without limitations.
Closing the gap. Converging on the ball. Match-up
rebounding.*

3. **BASIC RULES AND POSITIONS OF THE MATCH-UP   78**
Rule Play   79

When in Doubt . . .   80

Corner Position, Strong Side   82
Coaching suggestions.

Corner Position, Weak Side   83
Coaching suggestions.

Front Position, Strong Side   84
Coaching suggestions.

Front Position, Weak Side   85
Coaching suggestions.

Middle Position   85
Coaching suggestions.

Front-Line and Back-Line Adjustments   86

Middle Position to the Corner   87

Swinging the Front Line   91

Position Requirements   93
*Left-front position. Right-front position. Left-corner
position. Right-corner position. Middle position.*

Special Techniques from the Match-Up   96
Employing the senses. Blocked shot.

4. DEFENSING VARIOUS TECHNIQUES   102

The Overload   105

The Cutter   107

Switching on the Half-Court Weave   111

Trapping the Weave   114

The Screen and Roll   115

One-Three-One Patterns   118

The Low Post   126

Two-Three Continuities   127

5. MATCHING SPECIAL SITUATIONS   132

Defensing the Out-of-Bounds Play   133
Always defend the out-of-bounds play. Psychology is involved. Unnecessary to match-up every play. Let them set-up. Then match-up. Get close to the basket. Zone "jam" areas. Defending a screening from a weak side.

Developing Down Court Defense   140

Matching-Up or Defensing the Jump Ball   143
Key the jump. Verbal signal best. Only 20 minutes/ weak coaching time. Suggestions for the receiver.

Defensive Jump Formation   146

The Cover Jump Play   148

One-Three-One Defensive Jump   150

Matching-Up the Free Throw   151
The shooter. The rebound.

Obtaining the Ball   156
Cover the shooter. Blocking out from the inside.

6. **FAST BREAK FROM THE MATCH-UP** 158

The Specialist Theory 160
Location of the Players 161
*Best ball-handler. Right front man. Left corner man
Middle position. Right corner man.*

Lanes 164

Trailer 166

Tap-Out or Pass-Out 168
*One handed jump is higher. Tap to the top of the free
throw circle is easiest. Defending against the pick of
the play.*

Fast Break—Center Jump 173
Forming a pocket. The long tap.

The Quick Second Tap 179

Widely Used Fast Break Jump Formations 181

Free Throw Fast Break 182
From the made free throw. From the missed free throw.

Some Fast Break Drills 187
*Tap-out lay-up drill. Follow the lay-up drill. Three
line drills. The tap-out pass-out drill.*

7. **SCOUTING AND CHARTING** 194

A Must for the Match-Up 195

Scouting 195
*Area I—team patterns. Area II—individual information.
Area III—general offensive and defensive information.
Shot charts.*

Match-Up Scouting Summary 204

Charting 205
*A method of charting. Charting personnel. Uses. Major
categories. Shot charts.*

INDEX 215

Basketball's Match-Up Defense

1

THE MATCH-UP

WHAT IS THE MATCH-UP?

For many years, coaches searched for defenses capable of combating, or at least holding in check, the progress of offensive basketball. The increasing complexities of offense have brought about situations where the offensive attack is often more effective than the defense which has been designed to stop it.

Why has offense become so potent? A perfect basketball, standardization of floors, backboards and goals, improved lighting, and better coaching are a few of the causes. Defense, however, has had the same opportunity to take advantage of most of these advances. Not to be overlooked, of course, is the notable improvement in individual abilities and skills. The most important answer might lie in the greater emphasis today on pattern style play. We have more pattern play than ever, with new innovations being created daily.

Many continuity offenses have been devised to defeat

the man-to-man and zone defense. In order to adequately check one of the complex offensive patterns, the two basic defenses require some adjustment, no matter how minute, to function with maximum efficiency. Much time has been, and is still being, expended to introduce these necessary variations. The end result has been substantially the same. With few exceptions, the offense still enjoys an edge over the defense. Why can't the situation be reversed? Instead of emphasis on an offense to keep the defense off balance, why not a defense to keep the offense perplexed? In other words: "Let's put the offense on the defense."

The controversial zone defense has begun to overcome its growing pains. Coaches are beginning to realize that this type of defense has its merits and many have gone a step beyond the zone and created various combination defenses. Most teams use some variation of this type of defense in their attack today.

Regardless of the emphasis on pattern play, defense is gradually becoming important to the player, the coach, and the spectator, primarily because all of these participants have a better knowledge of the game.

Many successful coaches are not satisfied when they win a game in which the opponent has scored freely. This attitude can be supported by one of the new statistical categories in basketball. Team defensive prowess is being measured by the point ratio between the offensive average and the defensive average. In the past, team defensive average was determined by how many points the opposition scored. It is obvious that a ball-control team would have an outstanding defensive average on paper simply because they took very few shots, scored very little, and therefore, allowed their opponent very few opportunities to score. Obviously this would not be a true measure of their defensive abilities.

The individual player is beginning to measure his own defensive abilities very well. He knows his weaknesses and his strengths and realizes, through good coaching, how to take advantage of his limitations. Speed, strength, arm movement and position, foot movement and position, and other details of good defensive stance have been examined to give him an excellent analysis of what can or cannot be done defensively. Consequently, he may need help in some areas and he may be able to lend help in other areas.

The average fan seems to be losing interest in the high scoring game—probably because his understanding goes beyond the shooting of the ball. Today, the spectator understands team maneuvers to the extent of recognizing different defenses as well as the varied offensive patterns.

Personally, I feel that in most situations a good offensive player can defeat a good defensive player of equal ability with some help from a teammate. The screen, the cutter, or other pattern movements will make any defensive player vulnerable if his teammates do not have the ability to carry their share of the load. A development of this type would seem to prove that most individuals need help while on defense. Since offense is receiving help with the pattern, why not use the same theory and employ a patterned defense?

With the offensive player getting better and scores going higher, something must be done to equalize the scoring threat. One of the most evident answers is to spend more time working on individual and team defense. But, many times a team has reached its maximum in individual ability, while team defense does not improve a great deal. This problem usually comes about because team theory has not been developed.

Continuity patterns have been devised to defeat a man-to-man defense and a zone defense. The Match-Up defies

both offenses because it combines both defenses and produces an effect that cannot be solved unless special movement is created.

Specifically, the Match-Up closely integrates the rules of
good man-to-man and zone defense. It is a simplified rule
defense. The rules are simplified by using the ball as a
measure. (See Chapter 3 for basic rules.) With simple
rules, a harmonious coordination of all types of personnel
can be regulated to overcome the many offensive tactics.
The defense also takes advantage of the opponent's weaker
personnel and concentrates more on the strength of the
opposition.

Combines strong points of all defenses

The basic theory behind the moves of the Match-Up is
to combine the strong points of all defenses (both individual and team). Some of the team members will be
playing an aggressive man-to-man, some will be playing
a zone, and some may be playing a combination of these
defenses. These tactics evolve from a system of rules that
will make defensive play effective and intriguing. This,
of course, is a general statement and will be explained in
detail in Chapter 3.

These comments may seem to express what most zone
defenses execute, but let's take another quick look at rule
defense.

Many defenses utilize the idea: man on the ball plays
aggressive man-to-man, man on the man nearest the ball
overplays his man, and the remainder of the players zone
their area. These are proper rules with any defense; however, many problems will arise when the offense starts
moving, cutting, or changing position. With the Match-
Up, all offensive maneuvers should be rehearsed as they
are with any defense; with the rule theory, they will be

easier to handle as soon as a team becomes familiar with the controls that govern the patterns. A word of caution must be inserted at this point. Individual defense must be developed and the many defensive drills must be used to develop individual abilities.

One of the most interesting points of the Match-Up is that it can be operated from almost any formation. No matter what formation the defense may decide to start from, it will always move into the same pattern as the offense, meeting the individual demand of every offensive threat.

If the opponent stresses man-for-man offense, the Match-Up will combat this attack with dominant zone principles. If the opponent stresses zone tactics, the Match-Up will combat this with dominant man-to-man principles.

Defensive front changes constantly

In the Match-Up, new defensive fronts are constantly formed around the immediate area of the ball as the old fronts are constantly relocating to adapt to new situations such as cutters, screens, and overloads. Thus, the defense progresses by changing with the movement of the offense taking advantage of weaknesses and concentrating on the opponents' strong points.

No matter what type of defense a team employs, it must be able to combat the outside shooter, the drive, the cutter, the screen, and special situations like the big pivot man. Naturally, a coach is not going to be blessed every year with material that can stop all of these abilities on an individual basis. Consequently, he must exploit his available material to overcome any deficiencies which may confront the team from time to time. At the high school level, most teams have evident weaknesses, but with good scouting, weaknesses can also be found on the college level.

Very seldom does a team meet another in a contest in which all starters can drive, shoot, and make other good offensive moves. Most teams will have only one or two or, very seldom, three outstanding players. The Match-Up capitalizes on the weaknesses of the opposition, and puts the opposition to work trying to create something new. (The advantages of the Match-Up are discussed later in this chapter.)

Many teams are defeated because they are forced to do something unfamiliar during the course of a game. A ball handler may be forced to move in another direction, the pattern is not allowed to move freely, or a player is not allowed to shoot from his favorite spot. Since some teams read the Match-Up as a zone, and others will try man-to-man tactics against it, the rule theory of the defense will react by opposing each of these with opposite features of defense, as mentioned earlier.

There is no short cut to good defense, probably because it requires more time, more work, and more character in order to utilize its fullest potential. The rewards are not immediately harvested. The satisfaction that all beginning basketball players receive when making a field goal is accepted with immediate enthusiasm. A similar attitude of satisfaction must be developed in order to accquire the same results with individual and team defense. Rarely has a player learned to play good defense unless he has been taught to do so. A positive attitude on the part of the coach and the team should be an accepted fact. Knowing and using the individual fundamentals of defense must be a big part of the program. When these features are evident, the coach and the player will establish a balance between defense and offense.

In summary, then, the Match-Up is calculated to baffle

any offense. Because it is a rule defense, as opposed to the normal variations of the zone and man-to-man, a coach will discover that it will naturally adjust to various offensive attacks. These rules are easy to teach and master. For example if the left corner player knows the criteria for his position he will be ready to meet any offensive threat regardless of whether it's a screen and roll, a cut, a weave, or any type of zone pattern. In the long run this allows the coach more time for perfection of individual skills because the team theory is valid against any attack.

The Match-Up, as implied by the name, is governed by rules which enable it to "match" the alignment of the offense regardless of a changing pattern. In other words, as the offense moves, the defense will move into the same pattern without being vulnerable to familiar offensive maneuvers.

An integration of the best points of sound man-to-man and zone principles allows the coach to take advantage of the offense. For instance, when the opposition employs a man-to-man offense, the Match-Up combats with the dominant zone principles of defense. When the opponent employs zone principles, the Match-Up combats with dominant man-to-man principles of defense.

The Match-Up takes the appearance of a zone defense only to initiate the rules. However, the defense is located in a position to emphasize the effect just mentioned.

The Match-Up is not to be confused with the combination defense because most combination defenses are not formulated to adjust to continuous changes and are usually preoccupied with certain areas of the court or a specific pattern.

To get a meaningful conception of the rule theory which is the foundation of the Match-Up, refer to Chapter 3.

WHAT ARE THE ADVANTAGES OF THE MATCH-UP?

Effective defense has always relied upon the support of matching the offense with speed, size, and skill. With the man-to-man defense, the assignments are matched according to the ability of one player to guard another. The Match-Up defensive theory is very similar to the man-to-man theory. It will give a favorable player balance against the offense, but the placement of players many times is predetermined by the requirement of the position rather than the ability to guard a specific player. The assignments are made not only to stop the opponent but to keep good offensive and defensive balance. The defensive positions are coordinated and unified with this concept in mind.

Every defensive set-up is started with matched assignments. Guards will be guarding guards and, with few exceptions, forwards and centers will be guarding forwards and centers. This method is contrary to the man-to-man when the defense is called upon to switch. The switch many times will leave a small guard defending against the larger opponent under the basket or the slower, taller player defending against a speedier more aggressive guard away from the basket. When the offensive guard moves under the basket against the Match-Up, he will be at a disadvantage. The smaller front men very seldom go with the offense under the basket. They stay outside where they can cover more territory and have position to handle the fast break or set-up the offense when the ball changes over.

The big player stays under the basket where rebounding and shooting harrassment is practical. Many times it is difficult for one player to achieve these results and this is where team work is brought into the defensive scheme. Good individual defense is concerned with the shooter, but the methods used to score today are so effective that defensive team work is needed and must be perfected beyond ordinary demands.

Effective against individual strengths and weaknesses

A team's offensive strengths may consist of a favorite play or player that scores consistently—the big post man, the outside shooter, the versatile dribbler, the deceptive passer, and many other advantageous situations. Offensive weaknesses may include the absence of any of these on the part of the offense.

The act of disrupting a team by defensing against its strengths and taking advantage of its weaknesses has been practiced and used since defensive theory first developed. The methods used have not changed a great deal either. Over-playing a particular play or player, congesting scoring areas, double teaming, forcing the offense into a bad pass or hurried shot, have been exploited. At times some of the methods devised have been successful; on other occasions, they have brought disappointment. The Match-Up with its rule system can consistently and effectively handicap the offensive strengths a team may have. Following are some examples of obvious strengths of individual and team offense and the advantages of the Match-Up involved in these maneuvers.

The Big Pivot Man. Eighteen feet from the basket is a good scoring area for most players. It does not take a great deal of skill, ability, and practice to shoot from this area with better than average success. A logical conclusion then would be *to guard a player with the ball in this scoring area aggressively,* regardless of his abilities to shoot from other distances. Most big pivot men in today's game can shoot effectively, so they must be played strongly, employing the following techniques: they must be covered by sagging, double teaming, and converging. In order to stop the direct pass to a pivot man, a defender, many times, must play in front of him. It is difficult to stop the good pivot man after he receives the ball, but even if these methods fail to keep the ball from him completely, they certainly will curtail his offensive movement.

The Shooter. The jump-shot has added additional problems to guarding the shooter. Some shooters are so effective that it is almost impossible to lower their percentage from certain areas. Therefore, defense should be guided toward keeping them out of their favorite spots. The shooter must be made to force his shot with various methods of pressure defense.

Coaches have been saying for years, "One good shooter cannot beat us." This statement is true simply because five defensive players should be able to stop one shooter. It is understood that no team will be so poor in shooting that the defense can completely disregard the other four players.

The Match-Up works on the principle that some attention must be given all assignments, but advantages are taken when weaknesses are evident. This particular example may seem trivial but the desired results are not this simple. However, an uncomplicated view such as this may give the reader an idea of the importance of concentrating on the ball.

The Dribble. The dribble has always been a nemesis to good defense, especially at the end of the game when the offense needs to protect a lead. The dribble is most evident to the spectator when a freeze situations occurs, but it is probably more apparent to the coach when it is used to set up a scoring opportunity at any time during a game.

Techniques for combating the dribble and pass are employed by ordinary defenses with definite theory in mind.

This theory is common knowledge to most coaches. The Match-Up incorporates these techniques into the over-all scheme of team theory. A discussion of the advantage of these techniques follows.

When defensing the dribble, it may be desirable to force the dribbler in another direction, or to go after the ball with either a double-team defense or on an individual basis. From the Match-Up, several methods may be used with little adjustment. Since the dribble is not the fastest method used to move the ball, it will afford many opportunities to use various defensive attacks. For instance, on Diagram 23 we see an example of trapping the dribbler in the weave attack. Also, the technique of converging on the ball shown in Diagram 10 is an effective method of stopping the dribble.

The Pass. No part of basketball can be played without the pass. It is the heart of offense and one of the greatest problems of defense. A great deal of time is involved in teaching this part of the game because it is the quickest and probably the most efficient way in which to move the ball. Some coaches say that deceptive passers are born, not made. But regardless of how they receive their ability, they must be curtailed in order to win consistently.

The trap play once again comes in as an effective move to handicap the pass. Some traps try to steal the ball directly from the ball handler, while others concentrate on the pass made from the intended trap. Converging on the ball may cause a hurried pass, and if the hurried pass does not come about, this defense will most assuredly make it difficult. An interception is more likely to come about from a trap defense since the intended receivers will be overplayed.

Most of the time, a trap defense cannot be used throughout a complete game. Many times a coach will only use it at certain key opportunities. It may be used after a made foul shot or field goal, or it may be used to upset the style or pattern of the opponent at vital points during the game. With the Match-Up, the sides, corners, and middle are good trapping areas. These are all methods which can materialize with the normal process of the Match-Up.

Effective against a driving, screening type of offense

The driving, screening type of offense must be recognized as the most effective type of play in the game today. This method of play is used against any type of defense and will continue to get better. This is due mainly to the general improvement of individual basketball abilities.

Teams use the set screen, the double screen, the moving screen (even though it is a rule violation), or a combination of these methods. The primary purpose of the screen is to free the player with the ball so he may drive, have enough time to pass off, or have enough room to shoot. Options such as these present tough problems for any defense.

The reader may be asking at this point how the Match-Up can stop this seemingly potent offensive maneuver. Ordinarily the best defensive player is assigned to stop the best offensive player. Most of the time, however, there are not enough good defensive players to cover everyone sufficiently. In addition to this, there is another factor that may cause some concern: present day officiating somewhat favors offense. Thus, the theory of defensive help is before us and seems to be the answer.

In the Match-Up, as mentioned earlier in this chapter, if the ball is within accurate shooting range, the area around the ball is congested and the only possible use of a screen would be to afford an opportunity for the offense to shoot from the outside. On some occasions, coaches would be satisfied with this effect because, many times, the distance from which the shot is taken makes it ineffective. If, however, the shooter behind the screen must be stopped because of his effectiveness, fighting through aggressively with harrassment by the use of the hands, arms, and body is a must. Since the area around the ball is crowded, there is a better opportunity to take leeway in going after the ball.

The one-on-one situation very seldom arises near the basket against the Match-Up. This is where individual base-line drills that teach correct movement of the feet and correct body maneuvers are incorporated with the total program of team defense. The type of available material will always determine the abilities of defense from year to year, but regardless of the material the base-line can be closed off with help and overplay.

The zone defense was very seldom used, probably be-

At this point, there may be a general feeling of confusion on the part of the reader to accept the full value of these advantages if he has never been associated with a combination defense. Once the drills in Chapter 2 are mastered and the defensive rules in Chapter 3 are learned, all complexities should be erased.

Troublesome to the outside shooter

During the 1950-51 season, many high schools were running and shooting as the college teams were doing at that time. During this time, I was coaching at Hall High School in Kentucky, where the "run and shoot" game was the primary attack of most teams of the area. Very little attention was given to defense because the main purpose of the game was to outscore the opponent.

The zone defense was very seldom used, probably because of the influence that the University of Kentucky had on basketball in the area. When a team did employ a zone, a simple overload from a one-three-one formation would handle the defense adequately, simply because most of these mountain boys spent a great deal of time in the gymnasium and consequently were excellent outside shooters.

This season in particular, we were winning with regularity by outrunning and outshooting the opposition.

About half way through the season, we played Middlesboro, a team that was noted for its zone defense. We set up our usual one-three-one attack and felt confident it would handle the defense since we had beaten teams that had beaten Middlesboro.

During the first half of our initial encounter with Middlesboro, we could not get our usual open shot from the overload and went into the dressing room at half time with the score tied. Our fast break had kept us in the game to this point. During the half time, we decided to go with our man-to-man attack since it was obvious we did not have enough movement in our zone offense and we were not sure exactly what type of defense they were using.

We played a control game, at the end to hang on and win by two points with a very low total score. Man-for-man, we should have had a much better scoring team than Middlesboro, but as it was we were lucky to beat them.

Defensively they played us man-to-man on set maneuvers but zoned the screen and driving play. When we tried the overload, they covered the outside shooter so that he did not have an opportunity to receive the ball or have time to shoot if he did get the ball at these locations.

When preparing for Middlesboro a second time at the end of the season, we did a great deal of work on our zone attack. We used cutters to put two offensive players in a particular zone area by cutting into a new overload pattern. From this maneuver, if the short shot did not come about, a quick pass would get a good outside shot. We decided to screen the corners on the weak side since they were sluffing a great deal on the opposite side of the ball.

During the first half of the second game, we had built up a good lead and felt confident that screening the corners and cutting into a new pattern had solved the defense. During the second half, the opposition once again had made adjustments and covered our patterns and screens well. They shortened our lead by following the cutter to an area around the foul lane and then flaring out on each player tightly after our overload had been set. The area around the ball was so congested that the quick pass could not be made, which gave the weak side defense enough time to cover every player man-to-man. Once again we took home a very shaky win, but I felt we had been outplayed.

Sometime later, the coach of the Middlesboro team, Shelvie Fuson, informed me that he had inserted rules at half-time that covered our pattern, first with a zone, and then a man-to-man after the movement was completed. This move took care of our outside shooters.

Time is needed when working for the outside shot. Passes, dribbles, screens, and cutters must be used to free the outside shooter. This time can be used to get positioned to give the outside shooter trouble.

Without going into further technicalities at this point, the Match-Up is synonymous with stopping the outside shooter.

Effective for use of big slow men

The big, slow player probably will have trouble playing and adjusting to any type of defense. Nevertheless, he has his place on the team since the advantage of the "big man" outweighs many of the handicaps that he may present. When he is near the basket, he will give maximum protection in this area by making the short shot difficult to get. From this position, he will strengthen rebounding since he will be in a good place to go after the ball.

With the Match-Up, the big, slow man may be placed where his fundamental mistakes can be minimized, and with help he can play a great defensive game. Coach Billy Wells of Lenoir Rhyne College, after a long discussion on the use of the Match-Up, said, "Probably one of the best advantages of this type of defense is that I will be able to place my big man under the basket and know that he will not have to move to a defensive position that would put him at a disadvantage." This conception is just one of the many advantages, but it can be applied to any of the basic positions. In other words, *place a player where he is most effective.* He will have to move because no defense is static, but he will be near when and where he is needed. One of the advantages then, is the ability to Match-Up the opponent without fear of being forced into an undesirable defensive position.

Fundamentals can reach their limit when dealing with an individual who is handicapped with poor reactions and muscular control. This point is not made to give the coach the idea that fundamentals should be curtailed with the big, slow player because we never know how far a player may develop. However, he should always be used where he can do the team and himself the most good and fundamentals should be practiced as long as he plays basketball. The Match-Up takes advantage of this point.

Effective when you are in foul trouble

I have learned the value of the above message the hard

way. In the finals of the 1960 Florida State High School
Tournament, we were leading Daytona Beach by twenty-
three points at half time. Our fast break was snapping
with effect and we were scoring consistently when we
worked the ball from our set formation. Our defense had
done an excellent job because our big center was taking
up a lot of slack left by the corner players from the Match-
Up defense. Daytona Beach had a great scoring average
and the twenty-four points they scored the first half were
far below anything they had experienced all season.

We discussed this point at half time and set our plans
for the second half. Our center, who was carrying the load
in all departments, had committed three fouls. What
should we do if he acquired his fourth personal? We decided that a lead of twenty-three points was sufficient to
take him out of the game and insert him only with six
minutes to go or if Daytona Beach cut our lead to ten
points. In other words, he would go back into the game
whenever one of these options occured.

As the second half started, he committed his fourth personal foul. This versatile young man sat on the bench and
watched with the rest of us as they cut our lead with some
spectacular shooting. With exactly six minutes to go we
had a ten point lead. Our center went back into the game
to help us hold on. At this point our stall game was ineffective and our defense had fallen apart because the big
fellow was afraid to play aggressively for fear of obtaining
his disqualifying foul. We had put him back into the game
at his regular position. As the final horn sounded Daytona
Beach sank a long desperation shot to beat us. Needless
to say, we were heart-broken.

We had learned a valuable lesson too late. We had overlooked a defensive move that would probably have saved
the game. Our scouting reports had indicated that Daytona

Beach ran all their patterns or scoring attempts to the right. Had we placed our center at the left-corner position he could possibly have gotten a few rebounds, would have been available to give us our needed offensive punch, and would no doubt have helped with morale and team composure. If only we had put him in sooner at this location.

That was the only game we lost that year, but the season will not be remembered for the number of wins, only for the lesson, "When a key man is in danger of fouling out, use him if he is needed, but place him in a protected position." This can be done effectively and easily with the Match-Up.

Excellent for defensive rebounding

The movement of the Match-Up around the area of the ball creates many favorable rebound situations.

Since the players near the ball will be playing aggressive defense, they will be close enough to make contact with the opposition. Blocking or screening out is important before and after the shot, and since the man-to-man situation is prevailing in this instance, the fundamentals of rebounding can be exploited.

The long rebounder is the most difficult to keep away from the backboard. He can change direction easily and is in an excellent position to see and follow the ball. Since the defensive players under the basket opposite the ball will be sluffing to the backboard with the shot, they should be close enough to shut off the area so the long rebounder cannot get through to the basket in time to recover for the second effort.

Sometimes the offense will send their guards to the board for rebounding in order to outnumber the defense under the basket. This type of play would probably exist against a fast breaking team, but it has its merits against any type of defense. Most of the time the offensive guards are long rebounders. With the Match-Up, the area opposite the ball will be closed off six feet from the basket so these extra players should not cause a great deal of trouble from this particular side. The side of the court in which the ball is located will be engaged in man-to-man play and, therefore, should have rebound position since they will be on the inside. Many times the front defensive player opposite the ball will not have a specific assignment. If this is a fact he should be held responsible for front line blocking out. Many times he will not get a good clean block and may just brush his man, but the direction of the offensive player will be changed. This will use up valuable time which is needed to get into position to take the ball off the board.

Rebounding is not luck and the basic fundamentals of this particular phase of the game are reaction, aggressiveness, and position. Individual and team drills will improve all of these skills, both defensively and offensively. With the Match-Up, the bigger player is under the basket. This position should help in closing off the area and help keep the defensive rebounder from getting forced too far under. The rebound advantage should carry a lot of weight, for without the ball there is no offense.

Advantageous for fast breaking

The fast break requires a high degree of organization and basketball finesse. The many phases of this part of the game will be covered thoroughly in Chapter 6, but the advantages from the Match-Up are listed at this time.

The fast break from the rebound is probably the best and most widely used, and is the only type of movement we are speaking of at this point.

If the fast break is in the scheme of a team's attack, the

opponent cannot send all their players to the board for rebounding. Regardless of the method used to stop the quick break, someone must be in position to retreat down court. The best method is to out-rebound the opponent, but this is very difficult to achieve even with equal material since the fast breaking team is on the inside most of the time. Converging on the ball before the outlet pass is completed has been used with good effect by smaller teams. If one player handles the ball, some teams put pressure at mid court or at other positions where he may receive the outlet pass. Many teams drop back in a tandem at the other end of the court. Regardless of the method used to stop the break, the opposition must have at least one safety man back which gives at least one less rebounder to the offense. In many instances there may be two less rebounders since some teams send two players back in a tandem or keep them outside for this move until they see who gets possession of the ball.

Acquiring lanes from a man-to-man defense takes a great deal of experience, time, and work. The author has experienced only a few teams that could handle this with perfection. The fast break from the man-to-man presents many problems, but if they can be overcome it is a pleasure to watch and is very confusing to the defense.

The Match-Up simplifies many of these difficulties. The lanes are very accessible and several types of trailers are obvious along with the safety man, who should always be available in case of a bad pass or loose ball.

Effective against regular offense

Many teams are using a combination defense because it disrupts both the man-to-man and zone offenses.

When teams have comparative abilities the standard man-to-man, or zone offense, cannot get the job done against combination defense. Today, a team must prepare for three types of defense, the man-to-man, the zone and the combination defense such as the Match-Up. Many fail to prepare for the latter.

Sometimes coaches are set in their attitudes toward the defensive game. They use the same defense they were taught and may be very suspicious when it comes to ideas that have not been exposed for many years. Yet they will take pencil in hand and record every offensive pattern that is diagramed at a coaching clinic. That type of coach is vanishing because the progressive coach wants something more effective. He wants something diffierent so that he may disrupt the common offensive patterns. His defensive theory is sound because he has been exposed to the fundamentals that so many coaches missed.

Many coaches contend they would use certain methods in basketball but they would have to make concessions with particular phases of the game. For instance, some coaches in various areas do not like to fast break and lean more to free lance offense. Still others desire to fast break everything after a field goal including the foul shot, jump ball, and out-of-bounds play from back court. The Match-Up will blend with all theories since its primary purpose is to present a defensive plan that will answer the progress of offensive basketball. No implication is made or intimated concerning controlling other ideas of the game. Hence, team offenses will have to improve to cope with new problems of defense and this in turn will improve the game.

Effective on any size court

At one time, the home court advantage was worth more to a team than it is today. The small court is slowly disappearing and is being replaced with regulation floors and equipment as well as excellent seating arrangements.

Many teams have set impressive records with the zone defense when the home court provided a small, narrow playing area. Of course, the zone met with complications when they had to perform on the large courts. One of the strong disadvantages of the zone was advocated with the saying, "The larger the court, the less effective the defense." There is a great deal of truth in this statement especially if the team using a zone on a large floor is behind and must come out to force the game.

Many coaches stayed away from the zone because a team had to learn two defenses. Equivalent in meaning was the theory that a team could not have full confidence in two different defenses that were so far apart fundamentally. Much of this thinking has gone by the wayside because teams very seldom employ a single defense during one complete game anymore and good defense of any type requires exposing the player to good fundamentals.

The advantages due to the size of the court have been abolished in the larger schools. Most conferences have regulatory standards that must be satisfied. These regulations include floor size, floor markings, clock or timer, backboards, baskets, and many incidentals that formerly helped the home team. There are a few colleges and many high school gymnasiums that cannot meet regulations, but in ten years most of these will be replaced.

The large court is not a disadvantage for the Match-Up. The defense is very effective in the middle area and forces a team to take shots from ineffective areas. If a team should try to move the ball at a high rate of speed in order to get an open shot, cutting off the passing lanes would be one method of defense. However, it does not make any difference how fast a team can pass the ball because the offensive player receiving it will be guarded aggressively after he gets the ball.

From the Match-Up formation pressure can be put on the ball in the form of traps or just plain man-to-man defense at the half-court marker if needed.

A team that has both the man-to-man and zone defense in its repertoire may give rise to mixed emotions among the players. This emphasis on two divergent theories of defense may imply to the player that either of the defenses may have weaknesses since the coach changes defensive theory when one becomes supposedly ineffective.

There is no problem of such feelings concerning the Match-Up. The players will be familiar with all phases of defense and will gain confidence from the effective drills used to develop team tactics. The idea of working the defense against offenses such as those exhibited in Chapter 4 will exploit fundamentals to a point that team defense will become practicable.

2

BASIC DRILLS FOR
TEACHING THE MATCH-UP

Before going into the basic drills that make the Match-Up effective, the fundamentals of stance and footwork must be discussed. An inventory of the basic ideas of individual defense must be made in order to clarify some of the theory behind the drills in this chapter. Defense must start with the individual and eventually lead to creating situations that include the complete team. Teamwork, morale, and sound defense can be established by not leaving fundamentals to chance. Each step must be graduated and eventually lead to the complete process of defensive teamwork.

Several years ago, during my first year as basketball coach at Pompano Beach Senior High School, in Florida, an acute defensive problem became evident during the first few days of practice. When most of the boys reported for practice after the football season, I found right away that I had problems with defensive fundamentals. Very few boys knew the basic stance or foot movement. They were susceptible to fakes, left their feet at the slighest feint, and consequently were unsuccessful when trying to stop the drive. They could not move their feet satisfactorily because they had a tendency to drag them when sliding or shifting.

We had a short time to cover a great deal of defensive territory and it looked as though it would be an insurmountable task before our opening game. I had talked many times about putting a harness on various players in order to procure good body balance. The boys who could not keep their center of gravity low were in this category and were among the group having the most problems with defensive fundamentals.

THE POSITION MASTER

I discussed the problem with a local sporting goods dealer and mentioned my idea of the harness. We went to a local shoe repairman and came up with a device made of straps and elastic.

I used the device the very next day with our defensive drill. It was very easy to put on. I could put a player in the stance or position I desired by tightening or loosening the straps at the hips.

The second day showed drastic changes in foot movement. The elastic running to the ankles forced the foot up once it was removed from the floor with a slide or step. When the player placed his foot back down he had resistance. The pull and resistance acquainted him quickly with the idea of moving the feet. The resistance, when putting the foot down, made his legs stronger in a very stort time. The hips were kept in position because the elastic went from the back of the hips to the back of the ankles.

The over-all results were amazing. We did a creditable job on defense our first game. That year I employed a defense similar to the Match-Up and not one team drove the base-line for a lay-up.

Later, Aids Associates of Pompano Beach, Florida, made some improvements and gave the device its name, the Position Master.

I experimented a great deal with the Position Master that year. It was later used with our dribbling and conditioning drills. Over a period of years I have found that it will cut down defensive drill time because wasted motion is curtailed. The most stubborn bad habit can be corrected easily with its use. However, group and individual drills were and are practiced as extensively as ever.

With the group drills I desire to have everyone down at the same time and want them to stay down until the proper stance becomes a natural feeling. When I stop the group for individual correction, I am assured that every player will stay in position rather than rise up and relax. The Position Master allows freedom for foot movement in any direction and is not so forceful that a player cannot raise his hips when it is necessary to fight through a screen or to make other moves.

DEFENSIVE STANCE

Body position is the first element of defense. Without proper body position, body balance will not be uniform and the defensive player will be susceptible to quick starts, quick stops, fakes, feints, change of direction, and change of pace. Naturally, footwork will be handicapped without proper body balance.

Check defensive posture

Before defensive movement can be taught by the use of drills, the stance or defensive posture of each individual must be checked. With the young athlete, poor defensive posture will be easy to spot and improve. With the high school senior or college player, it may be difficult to detect and recognize over a short period of time. Minute errors of body balance, position, and movement will take more time for improvement because they usually occur with the advanced player. He is, more than likely, very set in his movement and must re-learn some techniques that have seemed natural over a long period of time.

Regardless of the experience or age of the candidate, I start from scratch at the beginning of practice each year. The basic body position involves several adjustments and I feel confident that my drills will develop each player properly once the routine of "getting down" meets my expectations.

Placement of the feet

It has been proven by experiment that parallel placement of the feet has its disadvantages as well as a few advantages. If the defensive player did not have to move backwards, placing the feet side by side would be ideal, but defense is required to move back more than any other direction. The degree of backward movement varies constantly and most coaches will agree it is a very difficult move to make, probably because very little of our natural daily routine requires this type of motion or activity. Therefore, I advocate placing one foot in front of the other—conventionally called the "boxer's stance."

Comfort, plus position should be factors in determining which foot should be forward. Since the young player may not know exactly what constitutes a comfortable position he should be observed closely and required to stay within the limitations or desires of the coaching staff. During elementary shifting or elementary footwork drills many problems will dissolve without a great deal of individual attention.

It would be ideal to have the front foot as the one opposite the direction to which the defense wants the offensive player to move, but there are a couple of reasons why this may not always be attained. Unless the defense already has good position before the offense receives the ball it is often very difficult to force the ball in a desired direction. Unless the offense pauses momentarily before making a move, difficulties may arise when attempting to achieve an ideal foot position if not already acquired. The theory of placing the front foot opposite the direction in which the offense is expected to move should be practiced with drills and is a definite advantage if accomplished. Ideally, all drills should strive for this position.

Role of the toes and knees

The toes and knees play an important part with foot-work and stance. If the feet are spread properly, usually shoulder width, many difficulties may not arise. The toes should form a natural position, pointing slightly outward. The knees should be flexed so that the center of gravity is proportioned correctly. (See Figure 1.) Unless a player has a slight deformity such as "pigeon toes" the foot should very seldom point inward. Occasionally a good athlete may have slight variations with foot placement because of defective problems that were not corrected during early childhood. These two instances are exceptions but nevertheless will occur. Many boys with minor foot handicaps have proven to be excellent defensive players even though their form did not look satisfactory.

The center of gravity, which depends upon the position of the hips, buttocks, and legs, is of utmost importance as it governs the body position. This, in turn, determines the performance of all defensive moves. The hips should be dropped with the knees bent so the defense can move freely without being hindered by the excessive weight shift which occurs when a player is off balance.

Figure 1

Many coaches emphasize defense by saying that it is played with the feet. The thought is very true, but the arms and hands should also be an active part of guarding. I always tell my players that the offense may think they have the advantage of knowing where they are going but the feet of the defense can cut them off and the arms and hands will be the equalizer; therefore we are virtually even with them.

Use of the arms and hands

Like all other phases of basketball there are many theories concerning the position of the arms and hands. Good hand position is important, but to introduce one type of hand and arm position for all players is similar to forcing every player to shoot the same type of shot. When all team members are mentally and physically alert to the proper use of the hands and arms, according to their abilities, the offense is presented with obstacles they do not meet in every game. The psychological advantage can be sizeable against a team that does a great deal of passing. Therefore, the use of hands and arms cannot be overemphasized.

Most coaches have formulated ideas concerning the position of the hands and arms based upon the defensive stance. Many want to mold the complete team into the same form. I believe the personal assets and limitations of the individual should be taken into consideration. The hands extended may be beneficial to some while the hands maintained close to the body may be beneficial to others. The reflexes of the individual are the determining factors. A basic position from which all movement of the hands originates should be formulated but the coach should allow for individual abilities as just mentioned. The position should be maintained in the initial stance and move from a point which produces the most speed, effect, and competency.

Blocking a shot is an individual matter. It would be ideal to have the hand that is on the side of the forward foot raised. But this entails such things as individual reflexes, the area in which the defense desires the offensive player to move or the ball to locate, and how the shooter moves the ball from hand to hand to get his shot off. A right-handed shooter could hold the ball at his left side while in a normal position. He could then shift the ball up to proper shooting position with his right hand. Thus, the defensive player would seem to be in a more favorable position if his left foot were forward and his left arm up.

The other hand can be drawn out to the side to stop a dribble or pass and will be in perfect position for an upward movement to bat or move for a loose ball. The upward movement, as opposed to a downward slap, will reduce contact and result in less fouling. Slapping down on the ball inadvertently results in many fouls regardless of personal contact. Many times contact may occur from the upward movement, but it is difficult for the official to call since the contact is under the ball and the hands.

The quality and character of footwork cannot be overlooked because its prominence is the foundation of defense.

No matter what type of defense is being taught, a proper approach to teaching the fundamentals of footwork must be developed. Today most teams have pre-season activity which includes work that prepares the feet and legs for vigorous drills at the opening of practice. Caution must be taken with the football player who is reporting late to basketball. Otherwise, aggressive foot movement should be started on a full scale at the beginning of practice.

DEFENSIVE IMPLICATIONS

Before physical activity, it is important that individual techniques of defense be mentioned to the player in order to set forth values that may not be brought out once actual drills are started. There is a definite line of distinction between being able to move properly and exercising the correct mental attitude.

A list of various hints involving individual techniques of stance and footwork is very practical and can be used constructively. The coach may use it as a checklist to assure himself that every detail has been included in the practice schedule. The list may also be given to the player as a reminder of the many individual requirements beyond the habitual or usual acts of defense.

Hints involving the proper mental approach, defensive position, and scouting methods are important when setting up drills that will eventually develop the team defense. Regardless of the method in which they are used and the number of times the coach and player have been associated with them, it is well worth the time it takes to associate the techniques with the practice plan.

Position hints

1. Keep knees bent and weight low.
2. Remain in the initial stance or crouch position as long as your opponent has possession of the ball. When he does not have the ball, there may be a need for a variation in stance.
3. Maintain body balance for the next move.
4. Shift weight smoothly from foot to foot.
5. Shift part of the weight to the bent front leg and foot.
6. When a change of direction is anticipated, do not play too close.
7. Practice the needed defensive moves (rolling off screens, fighting through screens, taking the short cut, etc.) which depend on a specific offensive move or maneuver.

8. Use the pivot to retain balance or position as well as outmaneuver the offense by working around a screen.
9. Develop abilities to go in any direction.
10. Body balance is needed when the opponent uses a fake.
11. Fake rushing-movement with drop-back is a good outside move.
12. Push off from the balls of the feet.
13. Never give the good shooter a deliberate shot.
14. Point to your man when an exchange is made.
15. When the defense forces the ball to stop, crowd the offense in most instances.
16. Correct movement of the hands helps retain body balance.
17. Do not leave your feet on fake shots or passes.
18. Occupy a commanding position and control the opponent.
19. Use the hands to hurry passes.
20. Be aggressive and develop proper body contact.
21. Do not cross the feet in a normal defensive maneuver.

Mental hints

1. Establish aggressive defensive dominance early in the game.
2. Use defensive fakes naturally—do not overdo them.
3. Anticipate defensive moves.
4. Be aware of the actor.
5. React quickly. Lack of decision will defeat the defense.
6. Maneuver with a purpose in mind.
7. Play defense according to the strength and weakness of the opponent.
8. Talk on defense—to the opponent and to your team.
9. Develop accurate, split–second timing through drills.
10. Spot offensive weaknesses with fakes.

Observation hints

1. Is the opponent fast or slow?
2. Can we give the opponent any shots? Where?
3. Does the opponent use a fake, feint, screen, or drive?
4. Is the opponent smart or mechanical?
5. Will the opponent react to defensive fakes?
6. Does the opponent have good vision or does he keep his head down?
7. Will the opponent charge or become frustrated when played tightly?
8. Does the opponent protect the ball?
9. Can the opponent change direction?
10. Does the opponent have an effective change of pace?
11. Does the opponent go after the loose ball?
12. What other abilities does the opponent possess?

FOOTWORK AND SHIFTING DRILLS

For effective development of the Match-Up defense, drills have been created or borrowed to teach the game situation as much as possible. These drills probably are not new, but they are necessary in order to take full advantage of the Match-Up theory.

Footwork fundamentals may be taught in connection with other drills. Change of direction is one of the most effective moves that can be combined with various passing, dribbling, and shooting drills. Since good defensive movement lessens body contact and since change of direction movement must be done without hesitation, many drills are effectively employed that involve several phases of basketball. However, in order to avoid repetition I will emphasize only the defensive drills.

Once the basics of a drill are mastered, it is a good idea to make it competitive. A challenge during practice has its place and is very interesting but caution must be taken. The purpose of the drill should never be permitted to get out of context. The intent of a player to beat his teammate sometimes causes distractions and the whole purpose of the drill may be defeated. It is always a good idea to quit at the right time so the proper attitude can be carried over to the game.

Best results are attained when specific objectives are kept in mind. The drills in this chapter are selected because they fulfill the following needs:

> They are needed to teach the Match-Up defense.
> They simulate the game situation as near as possible.
> A maximum number of players can practice with general defensive techniques at one time, thus saving valuable practice time.
> They instill pep and life in the practice sessions and lead to good team morale.

Directional slide and shift drill

Once the stance is corrected from a set position, the squad should progress to sliding, shifting, and other footwork drills.

In order to expedite the practice session it is best to work with the complete squad as a group. If a player is having difficulty with a particular move, individual work will probably be needed. He may be taken aside by an assistant coach as the rest of the group moves ahead with the planned drill. If the coach has no help he may work with the player during shooting practice or after the regular session is completed.

The late Cam Henderson of Marshall University, required every player to slide and shift at least five minutes before practice and another five to ten minutes after the formal practice session was completed. His team, year after year, proved to be excellent with the slide and shift from the two-three zone defense he originated. Once the basic stance was satisfactory he employed the drill as a conditioner instead of sprints or other maneuvers.

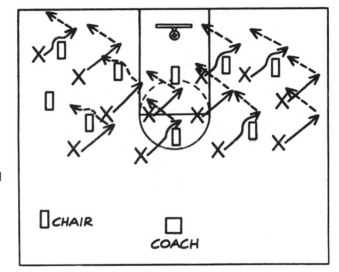

Diagram 1

METHOD

1. Create screens by placing chairs at various spots on the floor. Have the manager change the chairs from time to time in order to create new moves and new vision problems.

2. Place the squad in a convenient order but not in a straight line. Stagger player positions and have them interchange areas relative to the position they will be expected to play from the Match-Up.

3. The coach, the manager, or a player may signal the direction of movement with the hand. Later, for variation, have the group move with a dribbler as the leader.

4. Response should be vigorous and spontaneous in the direction of the signal.

5. Proper vision and movement against the simulated screen can be tested with various hand signals. The leader may employ a signal that requires the squad to return to their original position in order to check attentiveness and the use of split vision.

Start and stop drill

This drill is used to develop quick stops. Proper foot reaction to stopping will come about quickly from this activity. It must be emphasized at this point that the weight be kept low when coming to a stop. The drill should be used early in the season to develop correct body balance from a quick stop and may be used at any time as a conditioning exercise.

METHOD

1. Arrange the squad at the end of the playing floor in five lines.

2. Upon the signal the front row moves out to the other end of the court. On the next signal they stop quickly with arms and hands extended in the proper position and with the hips and buttocks low. On the third signal they move out again at full speed and stop when the signal is repeated at the discretion of the leader or coach.

3. Once the five men reach the base line on the opposite end of the court they will move back down court with the same signal procedure but will employ a backward movement.

4. At first it is best to use a whistle as the signal.

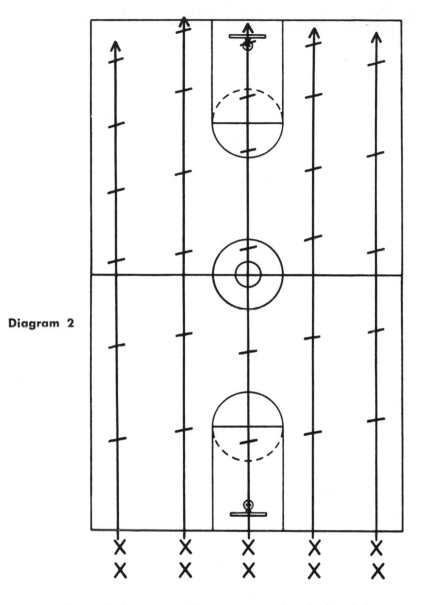

Diagram 2

Later it is a good idea to use a hand signal in order to assure proper vision.

5. After the drill has been used a few times the stopping movement will become a formality and most likely be in unison. Once the whistle sounds a

quick one-two count, stride stop, should occur. If this type of sound or action does not occur, someone is probably off balance.

Shift-slide-pass drill

The shift-slide-pass drill is used to teach the elementary process of lateral movement.

The drill acquires the best results when used during the early stages of footwork development. Later in the season, as abilities improve, competitive stages can be employed.

Close supervision should be given to body balance and footwork. The hips and buttocks will adjust easily to the correct position since the movement does not require a change of direction.

METHOD

1. The hands should be extended to receive and pass the ball. Although the hand movement is different from the requirement of defensive hand movement, the squad should form the habit of keeping their hands up and in front of the body. This

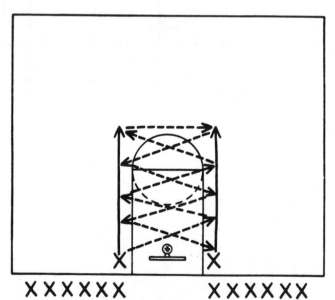

Diagram 3

hand position has a tendency to cause a player to lower his buttocks, which in turn helps him maintain the proper body balance.

2. Two players pass the ball back and forth while they are shifting or sliding to the top of the foul circle and back. The feet should never be crossed at any time during the drill.

3. For a competitive variation which will develop speed, each pair can be timed with a stop watch. Any violation of correct shifting or sliding would make the drill ineffective.

4. For an intersquad variation divide the squad into two equal groups. Have each group perform on separate ends of the court. The group completing the drill first wins the contest.

5. Another variation can be employed by placing a defensive player between the two players passing and shifting. The passers will have to change speed while the middle player will have to practice turns in order to deflect the pass.

6. For an offensive variation change the type of pass.

Rubber ball drill

The Rubber Ball Drill is devised to improve reactions that enable a player to stop the drive and move back to the original location after a pass-off has been made. The front and corner positions from the Match-Up are required to retreat quickly and move back to their original positions when combating the drive and swift pass combinations.

The Rubber Ball Drill exaggerates this movement on the part of the defense, but it is rugged enough to develop aggressive abilities such as those needed to stop the drive.

The drill should be used about once a week before the season opens and very sparingly during the regular season. It is an excellent conditioning exercise for pre-season and possibly spring training.

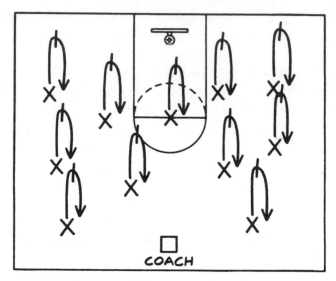

Diagram 4

METHOD

1. Arrange the squad on one end of the floor as shown in Diagram 4. Each player should have enough space to move backwards about six to ten feet.

2. Upon the first signal the group moves back in the same manner as stopping a drive play.

3. Upon the second signal they fall to the floor, face down, throwing their feet in the direction they were moving and catching themselves with their hands in front of them at the chest.

4. Upon the third signal the squad bounces up and moves to their original position with a quick stop using the correct defensive stance.

5. The drill is repeated several times. Caution must be taken by running the drill only a short period of time.

6. It is best to use the whistle as a signal when first employing the drill. As the group progresses a hand signal would be satisfactory in order to teach proper vision.

Dribble get-back-on-defense drill

This drill is devised to develop reflexes for changing from offense to defense.

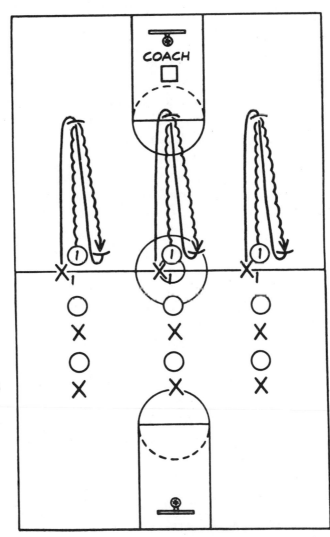

Diagram 5

Many drills have been originated to emphasize the change-over from offense to defense, but most of them cover the full court rather than the half court.

The Dribble Get-Back-On-Defense Drill simulates a situation that would occur if a team loses the ball offensively and needs repossession late in the game or at other vital points of game strategy. When a team is pressing full court a reaction of this type is needed. Agility, speed, and a quick change from offense to defense are the points to be stressed on an individual basis.

METHOD

1. Have the squad pair off according to equal size and ability.

2. The dribbler, (1), faces the basket at mid-court. His partner, X1, is to his right or left but half a step behind him.

3. Upon a signal the player with the ball, (1), dribbles half way to the basket in a straight line. The distance involved is usually about eighteen feet or from mid-court to the foul line extended. (1) places the ball on the floor and immediately takes defensive position on the ball.

4. X1, who started half a step behind the dribbler, (1), moves out quickly upon the original signal. He tries to get to the designated area before the ball. Once the ball is placed on the floor, X1 picks it up and endeavors to beat (1) back to the starting point.

5. (1), who started the drill, attempts to steal the ball from X1 after he has possession. If this fails, he then plays aggressive defense attempting to keep X1 from dribbling the ball back to the starting point at mid-court.

6. (1) and X1 exchange positions when it comes their turn to go again.
7. When first introducing the drill use only one pair of players at a time. Once the fundamental idea is understood, three groups may operate at one end of the court with enough room to develop the desired fundamentals.

One-two-three drill

There are many excellent one-on-one drills but the One-Two-Three Drill was developed to stop the drive and to challenge the ball once the drive has been stopped.

This drill simulates a game situation in which the defense cannot afford to give up a basket and at the same time needs possession desperately

During my early years of coaching I had trouble trying to develop a method that would teach a player to go after the ball, near the basket, without being victim for the easy lay-up. Over a period of time various experiments developed this reaction drill.

Defensive moves against the drive, holding the ball, and the pivot are the points to be developed from this type of activity. The competitive concept makes the drill stimulating.

METHOD

1. Have the squad pair off according to size and ability.
2. The offensive player, (1), has the ball at mid-court in a position to drive. His head is up facing the coach or leader who is under the basket.
3. The defensive player, X1, places himself in a close guarding position with his back to the basket.

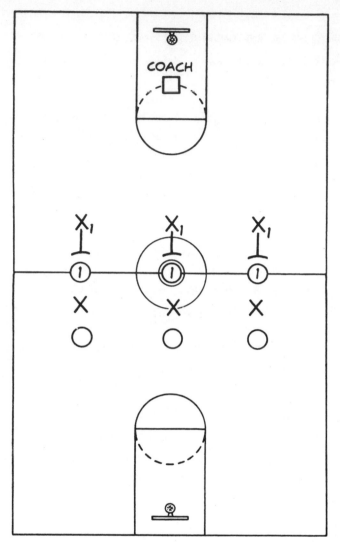

Diagram 6

4. The coach or leader under the basket calls the play.
   A. If the coach or leader signals with one finger, the offense, (1), will drive and try to score.
   B. If the coach or leader signals with two fingers the offense, (1), attempts to hold the ball directly over his head and protects the ball

with a pivot. Against this maneuver the defense, X1, endeavors to cause a loose ball
within a five second time limit by batting or
slapping at the ball.

C. If the coach or leader signals with three fingers the offense, (1), may pivot or protect
the ball in any manner for five seconds. Once
again the defense attempts to cause a loose
ball or attempts to tie up the ball.

5. X1 and (1) exchange places when their next turn
to participate comes about.

6. In order to expedite the practice session, once
the drill is understood, three groups may work
at the same time. If the drive signal is given, the
offense may use the other participants as a screen
which will make the drive more effective and the
defense more alert to game situations.

Three-on-three full-court

Coach Bruce Hale of the University of Miami has expressed many times the value of playing Three-On-Three
Full-Court. He emphasized at a recent coaching clinic that
it provides a strong incentive for developing most of the
methods and fundamentals of defense. Coach Hale has acquired his excellent reputation as an exponent of good,
fast-moving offense but he constantly talks about and uses
many good defensive drills, thus putting more emphasis
on defense than the average fan would suspect. Several
years ago I observed one of his practice sessions in which
he employed the Three-On-Three Drill to improve some
individual defensive problems that were evident at the
time. Later I began to work with various phases of the drill
which helped improve the abilities of the Match-Up.

Variations of this drill can be organized to teach any phase of defense and should be included with pre-season and daily practice sessions. Later it may be coordinated with the full-court defensive attack and can always be used as a conditioning exercise.

Full-court offense varies somewhat from half-court activity but most of the qualities needed to play good defense are exaggerated and exposed in a more strenuous form when working in the larger area. When the offense has more space in which to perform, defense becomes much more vigorous and is characterized with more speed than is required in a smaller area. Defense should then become less burdensome when applied in the front court since the offense does not have the opportunity to produce many of the abilities that the full-court allows.

With three-on-three drills I try to emphasize maneuvers that cut off the ball, double team the ball, force the ball to change direction, force bad passes, intercept passes, and provide situations that enable the defense to cover the opposition so they may not receive the ball. Once movement of the ball is stopped the opportunity to go after it becomes much less difficult. Fighting through or rolling off a screen, switching, and other tactics can also be developed to fulfill the needs of defensive theory.

Simply using the drill without a definite progression in mind would not insure good defense. The possibility of developing undesirable traits must be deleted by employing drills that graduate from simple maneuvers to complicated defensive theory. As a build up to the Match-Up and to teach many of the individual requirements of defense I employ three drills—the Short-Cut Drill, Three-On-Three With a Screen Drill, and then I emphasize Three-On-Three Without Limitations to the offense. The latter is usually employed regularly during the season.

Short-cut drill

"The shortest distance between two points is a straight line." This statement has become hackneyed by constant

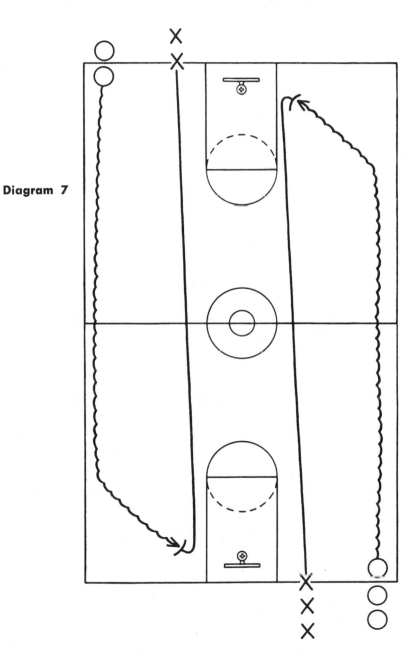

Diagram 7

use in all fields of learning but it still contains a lesson. How often does the inexperienced player lose his opponent and then follow directly behind him when trying to beat him to the basket? When this error occurs the defense must have greater speed than the offense or have some help in order to stop the ball. A point of good defense can easily be demonstrated by taking a short cut on the ball when it is moved to the side or away from the basket.

The Short-Cut Drill is used in order to develop the cut-off theory just mentioned. Many principles involved with stopping or cutting off the ball can be applied while speed and individual movement will improve.

METHOD

1. Divide the squad into two equal groups and place one group in the corner at the end of the floor.
2. Place the other group in the middle of the court under the basket.
3. On a signal, the first player in the corner dribbles for the opposite basket attempting to score.
4. On the same signal, the first player in the middle area moves out at top speed to cut off the ball as soon as possible, attaining a good defensive position.
5. The defensive player is not allowed to tie up the ball but any opportunity to cause a loose ball should be employed.
6. The defense should attempt to force the offense to change direction as soon as the ball is cut off.
7. The activity continues until the defense has acquired the ball, caused the offense to make a violation, or until the offense has scored.
8. Change the angle of approach by the offense and defense frequently.

Three-on-three with a screen drill

After the details of cutting off the ball have been emphasized the next step involves working against the screen.

No matter what type of offense a team may employ it will include screens that materialize on the side or from the rear. Practice sessions must include opportunities to combat these situations. These screens can be evaded by continuously feeling for the screen, by employing split vision, by constant talk, or by a combination of these tactics. Talking should be in the form of a warning concerning the location of the screener so the defense can make adjustments when he is not aware of such a predicament.

Without leaving his assignment each defensive player should take advantage of opportunities to help his teammate by deflecting the ball with his hands when the opportunity arises. These opportunities will probably occur during a hand off, when the player with the ball is stopped, or when errors involving passing and dribbling take place.

When an offense is weaving and cutting, such tactics as fighting over the screen, forcing the dribbler away from the screen, and many other points of individual defense must be developed. Many tactics such as these are sometimes overlooked when practice time is limited. High school coaches have the problem of getting their teams ready for the opening game with only a few practice sessions after the football season is over. It is a good idea to keep a defensive checklist when working with the simple fundamentals of defense especially under these circumstances.

METHOD

    1. Arrange the squad at the end of the court in groups of three. At first each group should be of

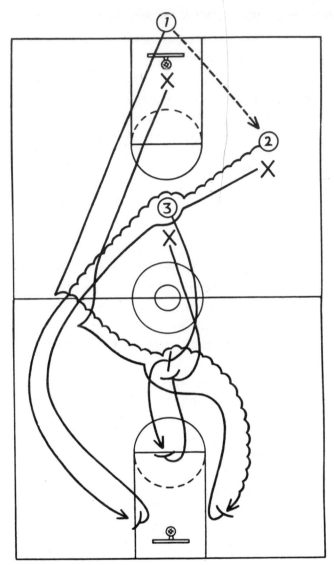

Diagram 8

equal ability, composed of a play-maker, a big
slow player, and a player in between these two
abilities. Later it is a good idea to have the play-
makers oppose each other, and the bigger players
oppose each other. In order to develop the big
men at a faster pace and at the same time build

morale, employ the smaller players against the big players occasionally.

2. One of the offensive players is designated as the screener and sets screens for his two team mates as the ball is moved up court. He does not handle the ball. The screening position is alternated each time the group is on offense.

3. The defense is not allowed to switch. They do not go after the ball unless it is uncontrolled by the offense, or until it reaches the foul line area on the opposite end of the court. Every opportunity to cause a loose ball should be taken but the defense should not lose their balance in an attempt to tie up the ball before it reaches the other end of the court. Proper foot movement, body balance, and position are points to be stressed.

4. If and when the defense does get possession of the ball, the offense takes the ball out of bounds at the side court until they progress to the opposite end. The two teams change over going back up court.

5. (1) and (2) handle the ball and (3) is employed as the screener. Allow (3) to move anywhere and set screens as the ball moves up court. It is obvious that the defensive men will have to be constantly feeling for the screen, listening for their teammates warning of an apparent screen, and then fight through or over the predicament.

Three-on-three without limitations

Now, the defense should be at a point where they can be let loose to use their individual abilities without a great deal of correction.

Once the squad has met the satisfactions of the coaching staff concerning the phases of defense that have just been discussed, any phase of defense can be worked out as a group with many individual problems already solved.

From this drill a coach can teach any type of team theory. He may desire to switch, trap, or converge and the basic idea behind most theories can be developed with the Three-On-Three Drill.

Closing the gap

Many teams read the Match-Up as a zone defense which is exactly what I want them to think. The zone attack is usually a strict pattern which leaves very little room for the individual stunting that will give any type of defense trouble. Consequently, if the pattern moves continuously in the same formation, defensive rules are not difficult to put into force.

The most popular, and probably the most effective, attack for the zone today involves placing an odd number of players outside against an even numbered zone and placing an even number of players outside against an uneven numbered zone. In other words the opponent will have an offense for the even numbered zone and another offense for the uneven numbered zone. A team using the even-uneven theory automatically goes into their formation when the ball is brought to the front court, once they take a look at the defensive alignment.

The Match-Up starts its defense from the two-three formation which inspires teams to attack from an uneven formation such as a one-three-one or a three-two. As soon as the ball starts moving the Match-Up will go immediately into the same formation as the offense and attempt to change as the offense changes.

When the Match-Up is switching or changing positions according to its rule set up, the offense will attempt to split two defensive players from the side or front. This

tactic is an excellent move and the defense must be prepared to stop the ball and then move out to cover a new
position when the ball is passed off.

When the opposition employs strict man-to-man principles instead of using the Match-Up we will, many times
for deceptive purposes, interchange to a straight two-three
zone defense. I have worked this from a key which may
come from the location of the middle defensive player, or
from an offensive situation such as a made foul shot or field
goal. Needless to say this makes the defense vulnerable for
the split position tactic. In order to prepare for this maneuver I use the Close-The-Gap Drill in Diagram 9.

Diagram 9

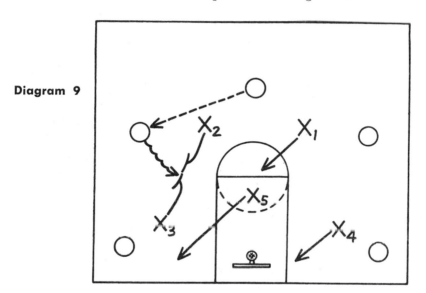

METHOD

  1. Place the defensive team in a two-three zone
      formation.

  2. Place the offensive team around the perimeter
      of the defensive formation splitting each position
      as evenly as possible.

3. The defense is not allowed to interfere with the ball as it is passed around but should shift and slide with the ball.

4. The offense at any time attempts to drive between two defensive players. If they do not get in a position to shoot they pass off to another offensive player who should try the same tactic.

5. Once the ball is closed off and the pass is forced out, the defense must hustle back to their original positions.

Converging on the ball

The opportunity to converge on the ball is another strong point of the Match-Up but like any other phase of the game it must be practiced and developed along with the many aspects of team defense.

Defense has become more daring and more imaginative because of the fantastic improvement of offense. Consequently, many teams are converging on the ball when meeting teams with abilities such as a strong pivot man, a one-man scoring team, a ball control team, or even a strong rebounding team. A converge may be used to keep the

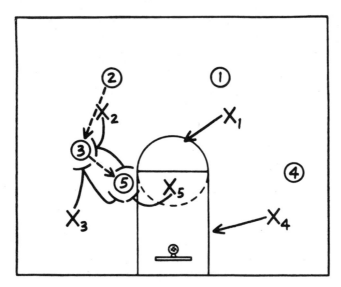

Diagram 10

number of shots down or to bring about more loose balls. Many times a converge is done with the full-court press when a weakness in ball handling is evident. Nevertheless, converging has many advantages but very few drills have been organized to teach this part of the game.

The areas most conducive to converging are the middle, the corner, and sometimes the sides.

A converge in the front area should be in the form of a trap which will overcome the weakness of opening up the middle or overcome the handicap of leaving an area under the basket unguarded. A good example of trapping or converging in the front area is explained in Diagram 10, which deals with the weave.

In Diagram 10 proper sliding and shifting should be emphasized from a regular two-three defensive formation.

METHOD

1. Set up the defense in a regular two-three formation.
2. The offense should be employed in various formations in addition to the example in Diagram 10.
3. When the ball is passed to (3), X2 and X3 form a converge.
4. Should the ball be passed to the middle, as diagrammed, X2 and X3 help X5 with a converge.
5. When the ball is moved into vulnerable converging areas, have the defense move in on the ball trying to tie it up or cause a loose ball. If the converge is not effective and the ball is passed to (1) or (2), the defense should move back to their original assignment and prepare for another opportunity to converge.
6. When the ball is successfully tied up by the defense, have them exchange places with the offense.

Match-up rebounding

Without going into elementary phases of defensive rebounding it is appropriate at this point to bring out team rebounding from the Match-Up. Before acquainting the squad with the primary and secondary duties of the rebounding team, each player should be well versed in the fundamentals. Much material is available concerning footwork, position, and other techniques, so I will concentrate on team theory with limited comment about fundamentals other than those discussed in Chapter 1.

The term block-out will be used in preference to screening or buffing in order to emphasize contact with the opponent.

Team drills serve as an opportunity to familiarize the squad with the positions of the Match-Up under simulated game situations. Opportunities to protect the base-line, block-out on the strong side of the court, block-out on the weak side of the court, and block-out from the front line, can and should be developed as a group.

Charting has an important place in rebounding and emphasis must be placed on tabulating the results. Chapter 7 includes all phases of charting with special interest placed on rebounding.

Blocking-out from the Match-Up varies somewhat from the man-to-man theory because players directly on the ball are responsible for an individual and the players opposite the ball are responsible for an area. Therefore, the defensive rebounder will have to formulate the habit of keeping his eyes on the ball and the offensive players in his area at the same time.

For many years I thought that blocking-out could only be done with a reverse pivot. A strong point that influenced me to use the reverse pivot was the fact that the foot movement was easy to formulate. My teams always seemed to do a creditable job with this method until we began to keep tabs on the block-outs that were missed.

During a conversation with Coach Glenn Wilkes of Stetson University several years ago, he informed me that he was holding each player on the bench responsible for keeping a mental check on a specific player in the game concerning missed blocks. In other words, the players not in the game would inform his assignment during a time out exactly how many block-out assignments he had missed.

With great enthusiasm I tried this theory at our next game. It met with only mediocre success the first night because the players on the bench were so involved with other game activities they did not keep a very accurate report. In addition we did not have a method with which to measure our results. Very little material is available about percentages on blocks missed because this is a relatively new statistic category. However, the idea became instinctive with practice and I came to the conclusion that we were missing many assignments that should have been taken care of with normal procedure. After some experimenting I decided the reverse pivot was causing some of our problems because we had to take our eyes away from the assignment too soon.

Next season I changed our blocking-out method to the forward pivot. This theory involved a cross over of the feet but allowed the rebounder to keep his eyes on the opponent longer. If the opponent goes to his right the prospective rebounder, with his back to the basket, moves his right foot across stepping in front of and making contact with the offense. When the opponent goes to his left the rebounder uses a forward pivot to the left. I am satisfied this is the most effective way to block-out for rebounding. Many times when good contact is not made the defensive rebounder can get in the way of his opponent just enough to throw him off stride which hinders his timing.

The forward pivot invites more contact but I personally believe that basketball is leaning toward more aggressive play. This particular type of blocking does not seem to raise the team foul total. Probably because more contact is allowed by all participants when the ball goes to the basket or with any type of loose ball.

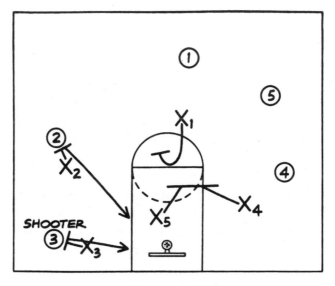

Diagram 11

Individual rebounding from the Match-Up involves the player on the ball and the two players on either side of the ball. The only exception to this rule would be when the front player is sluffing away from a weak shooter. He may then help form a wall around the basket in his area.

Team rebounding involves the corner player, the middle player, and/or many times the front player away from the ball.

The front line is responsible for the long rebound either on an individual basis or a team basis when the area under the basket is covered. Team situations usually occur when defensive sluffing is evident and the offense is away from the basket on the weak side.

The blocking-out and rebounding situations in the following diagrams are practiced from a stationary set up. Any combination of these rebounding moves will occur during a game situation and the habit of changing from an individual rebound to the various team combinations should be practiced until it becomes instinctive.

METHOD

1. X4 and X5 are responsible for the weak side area. They form a wall block since the offense is out from the basket and X5 is not involved with an individual rebound.
2. X3 blocks-out (3).
3. X2 blocks-out (2).

Diagram 12

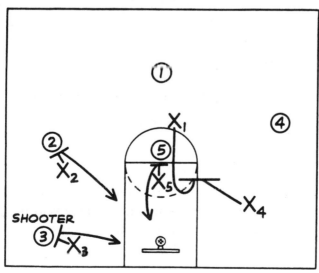

4. X1 is sluffing to jam the middle and is responsible for the long rebound. Since the area under the basket is covered he protects the area around the foul line.

METHOD

1. X4 and X1 form a wall block on the weak side.
2. X5 blocks-out (5).
3. X3 blocks-out (3).
4. X2 blocks-out (2).

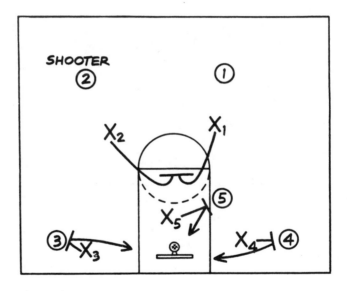

Diagram 13

METHOD

1. After the long shot is taken X1 and X2 form a wall block at the foul line. (The reason for this type of block is that the offense is located a great

distance from the basket. Conversely, if the offense is playing tight, individual block outs would be more effective.)

2. X4 may sluff some since the shot is taken on the opposite side. He is still responsible for (4) because he is fairly close to the basket.
3. X3 and X5 block-out (3) and (5).
4. Other formations can be arranged so the defense will have to block-out from different areas and with different teammates.

3

BASIC RULES
AND POSITIONS OF
THE MATCH-UP

RULE PLAY

The formation upon which the rules of the Match-Up are based is two-out and three-under. Facing the middle of the court, the two players away from the basket are designated as the left-front position and the right-front position. The three players under the basket are designated as the left-corner position, the middle position, and the right-corner position.

The 2-3 or "home" position may vary slightly but rule play should start relatively from these locations. If the offense has a high post man with forwards in tight under the basket, the defense will have the appearance of a 2-1-2 formation. If the offense places the forwards in the corners the basic formation would have a 2-3 appearance. These even numbered offensive formations are matched before rules of the defense have been put into effect.

The odd numbered offense, such as the 1-3-1 and the 3-2, requires defensive movement before it can be matched in the same manner as the even numbered offense. It would be ideal to go into the formation of the offense as they set up but the Match-Up operates with rules that are determined by the location of the ball. Experimentation with the Match-Up theory from the odd numbered formation has proven difficult. With a great deal of adjustment, it can be done. When the matching theory is employed from the odd numbered formation it requires a lot of teaching during the game which is usually difficult; time outs are usually not plentiful enough for defensive adjustment of this type. Defensive rules should be simple and short. From the odd numbered formation they become complicated and numerous.

The Match-Up will very seldom keep the initial 2-3 formation unless the offense stays in a 2-1-2 or 2-3 set-up; with offense as it is today, this very seldom happens. When a scoring threat becomes apparent each offensive player will be matched regardless of the original formation. The fact that the defense does not match the offensive pattern from the start does not present a problem. When the ball starts moving, the players start reacting with the rules.

WHEN IN DOUBT...

Several years ago when the Match-Up idea was new, my team would become confused occasionally when meeting an offensive pattern that was unfamiliar. Consequently we would drop back into the original 2-3 formation in order to close off the area around the basket and force the opponent to work the ball outside. As soon as we could formulate the rules again we would pull out and match their formation. The middle position was the key to relocating to our original position. He would yell "home" and the team would carefully move back to the original set-up.

The move was good for two reasons. First, it was excellent because we were not familiar enough with correct defensive movement and were unable to match-up all types of formations and patterns. The "home" position gave us an excellent opportunity to readjust. Second, it confused the offense. They were forever trying to change their offense to combat our defense and they were not sure whether we were using a zone or a man-to-man. In recent years I have discarded this theory although it has its merit. After exposing the Match-Up to the situations in Chapter 2 and the various offensive patterns in Chapter 4, confusion on the part of the defense involving changing patterns, cutting, and other offensive methods is completely abolished.

The general defensive areas assigned the players are important but more meaningful is the location of the ball. Stopping the ball is the objective of all defense. The rules are developed so they may operate on the primary target, the ball. The greatest problem will be to get each player to react quickly and effectively to the many changing conditions around the ball. Reaction to the area away from the ball is less demanding but takes speed and concentration because more floor space must be covered. Many hours of practice will be needed in order to employ all rules correctly.

Two main areas on the court must be defined even though they are familiar terms. One must imagine a line bisecting the court lengthwise. The halves of the court will be designated strong or weak, depending upon the position of the ball.

STRONG SIDE—THE AREA ON THE SIDE OF THE COURT IN WHICH THE BALL IS LOCATED.

WEAK SIDE   —THE AREA ON THE SIDE OF THE COURT OPPOSITE THE BALL.

Let's examine player position from the 2-3 set-up. Keep in mind that strong side positions can refer to either side of the defense since they change as the ball moves from one side of the court to another. Diagram 14 demonstrates player position and the strong side and the weak side of the court.

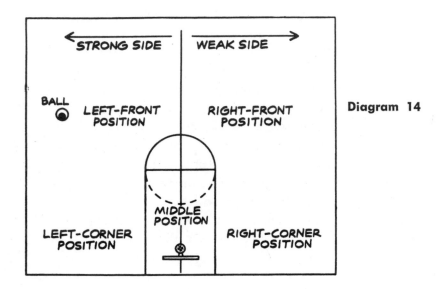

Diagram 14

Rules for each position are different but simple. The front and corner players must be familiar with the strong side and weak side rules. When the ball is on their side of the court they will employ strong side rules. When the ball is on the opposite side of the court they will employ weak side rules.

CORNER POSITION, STRONG SIDE

Rule: Defense the first player from the base-line nearest the side line, with aggressive man-to-man play.

Coaching suggestions

1. When the first player from the base-line is above the foul line extended, the corner position, strong side, zones his area. He must be prepared for the cutter to come into his area or help out under the basket.

2. When the strong side corner is involved with the ball, very seldom will he be able to move to another player who may cut from behind to the base-line or corner. In this instance, the middle position will move to the area to cover the new player. This move is discussed fully later in the chapter.

3. The corner player should always be prepared to cut off the base-line drive with good defensive foot and body movement. He should force the ball into the middle area of the court by overplaying the base-line. When the ball is forced into the middle of the defense, help from the front and middle positions is available.

4. The position is responsible for blocking out his man when a shot is taken since he is playing a man-to-man situation most of the time.

CORNER POSITION, WEAK SIDE

Rule: Zone his area by sluffing off to get good rebound position.

Coaching suggestions

1. This position will take over the middle position assignments when the middle position pulls out to help defense the strong side.

2. When the two front positions are needed on the strong side this position may be required to move out and

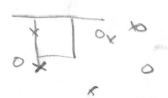

take a high man on the weak side. He never makes this move when a player is in his area near the basket, however.

3. This position is always alert to cutters coming into his area from the strong side.

4. If the middle position is high on the foul lane this position may be required to move across under the basket, to the strong side. The scouting report will help determine most of these situations. Moving to the strong side under the basket may involve the roamer from the 1-3-1 formation.

5. The lead pass is a threat to this area since the middle position overplays his position a great deal. Be prepared to sluff.

6. Rebounding from this area is done by forming a team situation with the middle position or the weak side front position.

FRONT POSITION, STRONG SIDE

Rule: Defense the second man from the base-line nearest the side-line with aggressive man-to-man play.

Coaching suggestions

1. If there is no player between the base-line and foul line extended, he takes the first man from the foul line extended. In other words the corner position, strong side, does not come out this far.

2. Cutters from this position should be overplayed on the side of the ball.

3. Overplay the cutter to the foul lane area and release him to the players under the basket. Move back outside looking for a new assignment which will still be the second player from the base-line.

4. The scouting report will determine most of the duties

of this position. If a player is not needed in the outer area, this position can drop back to the foul circle area and help with a converge when the ball is passed in the middle, or double team with the corner position, or double team with the weak side front position.

FRONT POSITION, WEAK SIDE

Rule: Defense third man from base-line around the perimeter on the side of the court in which the ball is located.

Coaching suggestions

1. When the ball is in the corner, aggressive play is usually not necessary at this location since there is usually a player between this position and the ball.

2. Zone tactics are necessary when the ball is not demanding aggressive man-to-man defense on the third player from the base-line.

3. If there is no third man from the base-line this position may help to control the following:

    A. Help jam the middle area by sluffing.

    B. Take a high man opposite the ball.

    C. Move under the basket to the right-corner position momentarily, when that position has moved into the middle area.

4. Rebounding from this area may be done on an individual basis when the offense is demanding man-to-man play or on a team basis with the weak side when the position is sluffing.

MIDDLE POSITION

Rule: Defenses the potential scoring threat nearest the basket in his area with aggressive man-to-man play.

Coaching suggestions

1. Play in front of the pivot man who sets up under the basket. The important thing is to prevent him from getting the ball while in good position. If he can't get the ball and can't score, he will most likely move out to the high post which is what you want him to do.

2. The lead pass is vulnerable from this area unless the weak side corner position is alert to help out.

3. When two players invade this area, neither one in possession of the ball, take the player nearest the ball and the basket. The front line will help defense the players located in the outer middle areas.

4. When the strong side corner is concentrating on the ball and cannot move to a new assignment, the middle position pulls to the corner if needed. This situation will have to be rehearsed and is discussed later in the chapter.

5. When in doubt, as a last resort, zone the area.

FRONT-LINE AND BACK-LINE ADJUSTMENTS

As you know, many elements of the Match-Up are involved with sound zone principles. Some of these involve stereotyped or fixed moves that are effective because they keep rebounding power near the basket and player location static when exceptions to the rule present themselves.

There are two general rules that will help clarify most of the adaptations required when dealing with the zone offense. The scouting report, once again, cannot be overemphasized. It is not imperative that a particular opponent's offense be rehearsed, since most of the known basic moves of offense should be matched early in the season, but familiarity with the opponent's pattern usually breeds confidence. As the rules become habit, reaction to most situations will become automatic.

When the back line of the Match-Up cannot make moves according to the rule, without granting scoring opportunities, the front line must adjust.

When the front line of the Match-Up cannot make moves according to the rule, without granting scoring opportunities, the back line must adjust.

When the middle position moves to the corner and the surrounding areas respond by making the proper moves, the three players on the back line have adjusted. If the two players on the front line swing with the ball when permitting the opponent to move the ball around the perimeter and relocate on the strong side of the court, they will have adjusted out front.

MIDDLE POSITION TO THE CORNER

Many times the strong side corner position will be involved with an aggressive man-to-man situation from a high position in his area. Meaning, he will be guarding a player who has the ball near the foul line extended area at the side line. While he is defensing this particular player, a cutter from the weak side or from the outside may move through to the corner. In most instances it would not be feasible for the strong side corner position to release the ball and move down to defense the cutter although he is rightly his assignment. The middle position moves to the corner to defense the cutter which is primarily a zone move. However, he will defense him on a man-to-man basis, forcing him away from the base-line if he attempts a drive. The exact defensive position will be determined by the scouting report. If the offensive player is an effective shooter and drives well, overplay may be necessary in order to keep him from getting the ball. If he cannot shoot from the corner and drives well, it probably would be a good idea to play some distance from him but close enough to cause a hurried shot. The latter location allows a better rebound situation in which the middle position can take advantage of his height and size.

It is apparent when the middle position moves to the corner that a player of comparative size and ability is needed to take his place. The weak side corner position is the defensive player who makes the move. Since the ball is opposite him he should be near and the exchange will be simple.

Many times the weak side front position will be available to help "jam-up" the middle if the ball is passed to this area successfully. The weak side corner may need some help at this point—either in the middle area involving the opposing center or momentarily in the weak side corner position. As shown in Diagram 15, the weak side front position is sluffing to the foul line and is the logical player to move under the basket or move to the corner if needed. He should have time to make these moves since the ball must be worked to this area.

Most coaches want to keep the "big" defensive center in the middle as much as possible in order to take advantage of his size. However, when he is forced to move to the

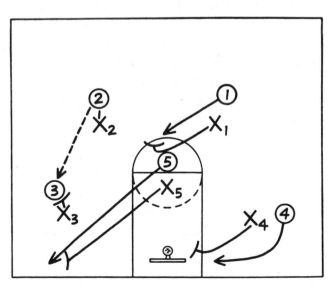

Diagram 15

corner, he is not so far away that he cannot get good rebound position. In addition, the opposite corner player fills in the middle position and he most likely will be of comparable size with the offensive player cutting under the basket.

When the strong side corner position is not required to play his position aggressively he may easily slide down and take the cutter who has moved to the corner. When he moves to defense the corner, the front position on the strong side will have to move down and replace him. Neither of these moves should be difficult since the player to be covered is obviously no threat as an outside *shooter* in this instance.

It is not important that the reader agree with this move. Material will vary and the coach must make adjustments accordingly. The existing offense will determine the selection and rejection of various defensive tactics. Over the years this move has proven very effective with the Match-Up.

The exchange of positions should be rehearsed like a one act play until the moves become spontaneous.

METHOD

1. X2 and X3 cover (2) and (3) tightly since there is no movement from these positions.
2. X4 covers (4) by playing in front of him. He will also protect the middle by moving near the foul lane.
3. X5 covers (5) as he moves to the corner. (NOTE: Since X3 is covering (3) who has the ball, the rule exception of pulling the middle position to the corner is in effect.)
4. X1 covers (1) by playing in front of him. He also helps cover the middle area since X5 has moved to the corner.

A cut to the corner can start from various positions. Diagram 16 deals with the opposite forward moving across the court. Other offensive cuts can be organized with a similar defensive maneuver involved.

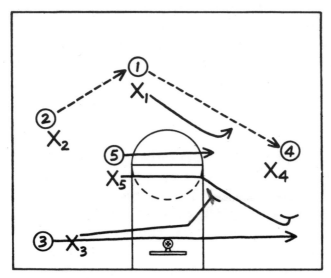

Diagram 16

METHOD

1. Set up the defensive team in a regular two-three formation.
2. The offense may set up in any formation but one of the players must eventually cut to the corner on the side of the ball. The formation in Diagram 16 starts with an even numbered set up, two-three, but moves into a one-three-one.
3. X2 moves up to play the ball aggressively.
4. When (3) cuts through to the corner X3 overplays him until he reaches the middle area and switches with X5 who is guarding (5).

5. X5 picks up (3) and moves to the corner with him since X4 cannot release the ball and move to take what would ordinarily be his assignment.
6. X4 covers (4) aggressively.
7. X1 has the option of sluffing to the middle or moving over to guard (1).
8. If a new cut is made to the opposite corner the interchange is made in the same manner. Usually the defense will have an opportunity to readjust to the normal set-up if the ball moves to the outside.

SWINGING THE FRONT LINE

A play that requires the front line defense to swing to the opposite side of the court usually involves a cutter that is not or cannot be challenged by the back line.

When a cutter is not involved, swinging the front line is simple. As the ball is allowed to be moved around the perimeter the front line is usually sluffing and moving. In this instance it is not difficult to put the rule play into effect because the defense is taking a short cut on the ball by sliding across the top of the circle.

If the front line is involved with a cutter, particular attention must be given to the offensive movement so the swing can be made without causing an area to be left open or a player unguarded. The cutter must be overplayed on the side of the ball to the foul line area and adjustments made to cover the opposite side of the court which will become the strong side and in all probability involve the cutter who moved to the side of the ball. If the weak side corner is involved deep in his territory it is the duty of the front line to handle the outside shooters.

Remember, when the front line must play aggressively outside, the back line will probably have to do the adjusting. If the front line can sluff and allow the ball to be moved around the perimeter, they will do the adjusting themselves.

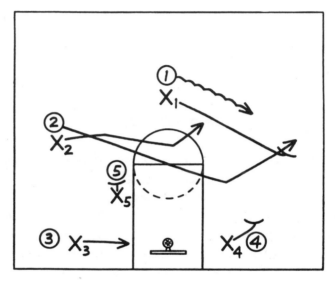

Diagram 17

METHOD

1. X2 overplays (2) to the foul line area, releases him and slides across covering (1).

2. X1 follows (1) loosely as he dribbles looking for a receiver to move to the side. When (2) cuts through X1 covers him releasing (1) to X2.

3. X5 is involved with aggressive man-to-man play on (5).

4. X4 is involved with aggressive man-to-man play with (4).

5. X3, as the ball moves to the opposite side of the court, sluffs toward the basket.

POSITION REQUIREMENTS

If ideal defensive abilities could be developed each season a coach would not bother much with defensive theory. He would play a straight man-to-man and handle any pattern without fear of being easily scored upon. Of course the conception of individual abilities reaching ideal perfection each year is beyond the realm of logic. Consequently, the coach must adjust his material in order to achieve the best team effort from the entire group. A particular player may have slow foot movement, another may be a poor rebounder, and still another may be inexperienced. At the same time the coach may be blessed with boys that can carry more than their share of the defensive load. Blending the strong points with the weak points into a smoothly working combination is one of the interesting challenges of coaching. Offensively one or two boys may work by themselves and score freely. Defensively a weak player cannot be left to haphazard play; he must have help or the game will be broken wide open because it doesn't take long to discover poor defense. These are reasons why a listing of the duties and requirements of the Match-Up positions is needed.

Arrangement of these items is based upon the practical needs of team defense. A plan is presented and the coach should select or reject as he sees fit. Finally, the coach may take parts and insert his own ideas or improvements to develop his own concept with the material he has available.

We will assume that the coach realizes the offensive potential of the Match-Up. Hence, I have suggested in the following position requirements some fast break criteria which are expanded further in Chapter 6.

Left-front position

The best of the smaller players should be located in this area. Speed is important since he will probably have to carry more of the load of the front line work.

If the fast break is employed from the tap-out, the man in this position will be required to use the various screening methods listed in Chapter 6. Therefore, in addition to needed ball handling abilities, he should be the stronger of the two front players.

Most teams are predominantly right handed and will have a tendency to run their offense in the direction of the left-front position which demands more movement and vigorous activity from this area.

Duties: Closing the gap with the left-corner position or the right-front position, overplaying cutters until they are released to another area, converging on the ball with other positions, fighting over screens, riding the roller after a successful screen and releasing him to another area, and trapping with the corner or right-front positions.

Right-front position

The slower, weaker, smaller, of the front players should be located in this area.

If the fast break is employed he should be right-handed in order to use his natural hand on the shot off the break. He should develop a short jump shot for the tail end of the break when it is stalled.

His general duties are the same as the left-front position listed above.

Left-corner position

Ideally, he should be left-handed and the best all around big boy on the team. Speed and agility are needed to fill the third lane of the fast break from this area. Generally this area requires a stronger more experienced player than the right-corner position. All back line positions should be the better rebounders on the squad.

Duties: Stop the base line drive, close the gap with the left-front position, converge with the middle and front positions, trap with the front position, and overplay cutters until they are released to another area.

Right-corner position

This is an ideal location for the big slow player. Rebound abilities are needed from this area. If he is blessed with speed he could be employed as a trailer. The primary duty after the rebound is the safety position when the ball changes from defense to offense. The inexperienced player or a player who is in danger of fouling out could play this position more adequately.

The general duties are the same as those of the left-corner position which are listed above.

Middle position

The best rebounder on the team should be located in this area since he will have an opportunity to rebound on all shots. Size and ruggedness will be needed from this area since the offense will be charging the board.

This position should be fundamentally sound with the defensive traits of guarding the pivot-man on a man-to-man basis. In other words, he should have the best individual defensive abilities of the big men on the team.

If he does not have fast break abilities one of the other

back line positions can be designated as the trailer in his place although this is the ideal location.

Duties: Aggressive individual play against the pivot-man, overplay from the middle area, picking up cutters as they move through the area, pulling to the corner area, converging with other positions, protecting the basket when the team is trapping, and cutting off any driving threat that may have escaped through other areas such as the base-line.

SPECIAL TECHNIQUES FROM THE MATCH-UP

Expert performance with the methods that follow has been witnessed year after year in basketball. There are many movements that may complement these techniques but time is valuable during the practice session. I have found it better to be expert in a few important abilities rather than mediocre in many methods.

Following are some methods that work well with the zone but the Match-Up exploits them to the fullest extent.

Employing the senses

The faculties employed to perceive the external objects of basketball usually separate the outstanding athlete from the average athlete. The senses of sight, hearing, and touch have been lauded by the offensive coach but very little material is available concerning their use and effectiveness defensively. Thinking, feeling, sound perception, and sight perception are all involved with reasoning and judgment. These senses can be extended beyond the realm of daily ordinary demands by employing drills that develop their reaction to game situations.

Peripheral vision development is a must in all phases of basketball. However, most attention is focused on the ball handler who seemingly has eyes in the back of his head because he makes a deceptive pass without looking directly at the receiver. If time would be taken to observe this same player while he is playing defense he probably would not be looking directly at the ball. Let a pass or loose ball challenge his position and the same result would be apparent defensively.

Each player should be taught to focus his attention primarily on the ball but he should be equally cognizant of the man or men in his area of defense. Peripheral vision drills that involve more than one ball are the most desirable used to teach this effect.

A drill created by Florida State University Coach, J. K. "Bud" Kennedy named Call Ball will help teach techniques of this type. The drill involves two balls. The players are scattered on half of the court with instructions to keep moving. They are assigned a player to pass the ball to. When the passer receives the ball his assigned receiver yells his name. Without dribbling or traveling the player in possession of the ball locates his receiver by employing peripheral vision and/or head movement and makes a sharp pass to him. The drill necessitates concentrating on the assigned passer, two balls moving in various directions, and player movement. They must be careful not to bump into the other participants.

A two-ball drill, sometimes called Pepper The Post, is commonly used to get a similar effect. A semi-circle is formed around the receiver who is located about twelve feet away. As the receiver passes the ball to a player in the semi-circle another player simultaneously passes another ball to him.

Any type of a "keep away" drill will help develop the same effect. There are many familiar drills which involve one group keeping the ball from a player or a group of

·players. The circle drill that places five players around the free throw circle and one player in the middle who tries to touch the ball as it is being passed back and forth is an excellent example of "keep away."

Although I have no scientific proof to support the assumption, I believe it is almost impossible to improve the peripheral vision of some boys. Eye defects and reaction handicaps may be the reason. The above statement does not imply that vision drills are not recommended for the seemingly handicapped. When a boy does not have good lateral vision, the employment of drills directed at these weaknesses does not necessarily lead to the development of better sight, although this is the desired effect. Drills of this type also produce needed improvement in head movement and general body reaction. Consequently, a boy can overcome sight handicaps with body adjustment.

The use of talk with defense goes hand-in-hand with deceptive vision. It is important that players talk constantly so that the men out front can be made aware of the position and movement of the players in back of them. It should be used to alert teammates of impending picks or screens which develop out of their field of vision at any position. Many times while a rear screen may be forming on a player in the front line, a player in the back line is in perfect position to call the move, thus averting a foul or deceptive offensive move.

The Match-Up is more effective when every player commands his position as if he were a traffic policeman. As movement of the offense develops he should point to his assignment and direct his teammate to the proper position. When releasing a cutter to another area talk is imperative. Statements such as "Cutter coming through!", "Get the second man from the base line!", "Rear Screen!", "Converge!", "Close the gap!", "Sluff!", and other descriptive information are associated with good team defense. The ears, the eyes, and the voice are important defensive weapons when developed properly. These techniques will strengthen a defense immeasurably and they are a great morale builder.

There is another slant on the use of talk with defense. In the 1962 Oglethorpe Invitational Tournament, Newberry College was playing the host team in the first round of play. At half time the score was very close and the game had proceeded without special incident. At the beginning of the second half Oglethorpe began to harass us with arm movement and verbal gestures when playing defense. I immediately called time out in order to settle the boys down. I attempted to impress upon them the value of concentrating upon their offensive duties rather than the action of the opponent. Whether or not this strategy, on the part of Oglethorpe, beat us in the closing minutes I do not know but it forced us to call a time out and adjust. Over the years I have seen players falter under verbal harrassment. The legality and ethical points of this type of play have been discussed at clinics on many occasions without definite conclusions. There is no rule against it as long as profanity and personal inflictions are not involved. Personally I think it has its place in the game. If the opponent has any indication of "rabbit ears" then take advantage of the weakness.

We know that a defensive player is never supposed to get caught completely out of position but it does happen. In this instance, talking defense is better than no defense at all and it works often enough to make it part of the game.

Touch is usually associated with offense but use of the hands on the part of the defensive player has become an art. Feeling for the screen, feeling for an assignment, directing a teammate, feeling to locate the position of the opponent from the pivot position, and using the arms and hands to move through a moving play are techniques that should be developed with any defensive theory. Regardless of the occasional foul that over-aggressiveness may cause, the Match-Up thrives on the use of the senses.

Blocked shot

During my first few years of coaching I did not include blocked shots in my charting because I was hesitant in demanding success in this department. Once the defender leaves his feet to block a bluffed shot, in most instances, he is at the mercy of the player with the ball. Fouls are committed and easy baskets are permitted when the defender leaves his feet before the offense has definitely committed themselves. Occasionally a boy with the natural instinct and timing to block shots comes along but generally a technique such as this must be developed from drills that invoke fakes and feints.

When an attempt is made to block a shot the defensive player should move in as close as possible before committing himself. Jumping with the arms extended above the defensive man's head is desirable. It is not absolutely necessary that the defense actually get a piece of the ball in order to force the shooter to make a split second adjustment with the arc and distance of his shot. An aggressive move, regardless of ball contact, causes higher percentage of error in shooting.

The Match-Up favors the blocked shot attempt. No drill will make every boy fake proof but if the dribble has been completed and the passing lanes have been cut off, chances can be taken that would not ordinarily be attempted. The zone principle of the Match-Up equalizes errors in defensive poise by adjusting from other areas. Encouraging the blocked shot by keeping statistics and developing the theory with proper drills is a needed technique of defense.

4

DEFENSING
VARIOUS OFFENSES

The day of the multiple offense is with us and it is important for all teams to be in a position to cope with many pattern variations. Of course, the ideal defense is one which will work equally well against all offenses which usually involve the screen, the cutter, the overload, and the many other continuity options. Matching-Up the various offenses is a vast step toward realization of this ideal.

Once the fundamentals of individual defense are skillfully gained, theory problems associated with team defense should be attempted. The importance of defensive fundamentals cannot be overemphasized since they are the foundation of guarding against the opponent's attack. The Match-Up is no exception to this theory. (Orientation of the materials in Chapter 3 is imperative before attempting the situation problems in this unit.)

Often teams change defense many times throughout a game. They may use different zones, the man-to-man, or possibly a trap or press defense. To the casual observer this may seem simple. But in the past, when this maneuver was handled skillfully, it meant that a team had to put in a great deal of time learning many different defenses and then adapting to a particular offense for each game it played. The team work of the Match-Up can curtail much of this extra work with its rule simplicity and easy adjustment. It is always easier when the situation has been rehearsed, but the problems can be adjusted as they are encountered.

It is common knowledge, but important, that a coach be ready with a set plan for teaching team defense. When this is done, many of the offensive options which will be encountered during the year can be prepared for before the season opens.

Offensive patterns that are anticipated should be explained and reviewed so that each player will clearly understand the defensive movement and other complications which will be necessary. Diagrams of these offensive patterns should be made early and copies given to each team member so they may be studied in preparation for group discussion and much valuable practice time can be saved.

The coach will find that the ability to prepare for opponents will vary little from game to game if offensive options have been reviewed early in the season.

The tactical situations discussed in this chapter are chosen because they have been used, with some success, against the Match-Up defense.

Some fundamental patterns are broken down into simple components so the defense may be seen in operation from a less complex viewpoint. The continuity offenses are more intricate and involve a great deal of movement on the part of the defense.

THE OVERLOAD

Very seldom will a team try to enforce a simple overload attack against the Match-Up. The results of such an attack are obvious. The limited offensive movement could easily be covered and it is apparent the offense would not get the easy open shot which it achieves against the zone defense. However, this tactic is tried on occasion, but is easily matched and double teamed if desired.

In the event that a team reads the Match-Up as a straight zone, the offense may attempt a stationary overload. When this simple overload is matched, naturally the offense will have to employ other maneuvers.

Diagram 18 may seem very simple and easy to match but the defense must have an opportunity to get acquainted with situations similar to the stationary overload in order to learn the theory behind the Match-Up. In a normal game situation a match-up of this type of offense probably occurs only in the early stages of the game since the offense will realize a need for some type of cutting or free lancing.

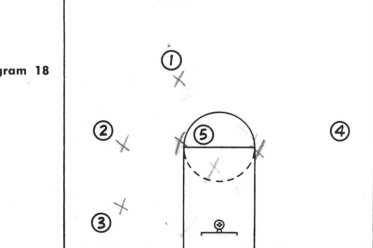

Diagram 18

As stated earlier, the Match-Up has many of the zone features incorporated in its attack. Only the rudimentary elements of the Match Up defense are needed to stop the overload. The offense is shown in Diagram 18 and the defensive positions shown in Diagram 19, so future adaptations may be simplified.

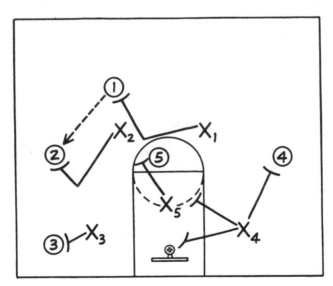

Diagram 19

METHOD

1. If (1) is an offensive threat, X1 covers him aggressively. He has the alternative to help cover (5), and at the same time stop-up the middle, or double team the ball if he is not needed to control (1). Note that the basic rule is in effect since (1) is the third player from the base-line.

2. The second offensive player from the base-line is (2). He is guarded tightly and aggressively by X2. X2 can aggravate the activity and accuracy of (2) by using his hands, arms, and body in an attempt

to cut off the passing lanes to the probable scoring threats who are (3) and (5).

3. Since (5) is in a good scoring position he must be covered aggressively by X5. A tight man-to-man defensive play on the side of the ball is the best maneuver. If either (2) or (3) moves past his defense for a drive, X5 is alert to cut them off or help wherever he is needed. Many times X5 may play in front of (5) if he is an effective shooter from this area. Note that X4 is in position to sluff-off should X5 need help because of a possible lead pass over his head from (2) or (3).

4. Threat nearest the base line is player (3) who must be covered by X3. If a drive is attempted, with the ball in possession of (3), X3 must then force him into the middle of the Match-Up which is toward the foul lane.

5. Player (4) is covered loosely by X4 when (2) has possession of the ball. The shooting and driving abilities of (4) will be factors involved when deciding exactly how (4) should be covered. Naturally, if the ball is moved to his side of the court (4) would be covered closely.

THE CUTTER

The cutter or give-and-go maneuver involves a pass to a teammate, a fake, and a quick move to the basket. In order for this play to be effective there must be an open area, and the play requires extreme skill and finesse.

A lot of timing and talk is involved in stopping the effectiveness of this move. The cutter must be covered while he is in a position to receive the ball, especially if he is a particularly good shooter. The defense should play in front of the cutter as much as possible. In other words, he should stay between the cutter and the ball. The defense is sus ceptible to a possible lead-pass in this position. However, the middle defensive position can assist in most cases. The scouting report should list the liberties which may or may not be taken.

When the defense is in doubt as to the individual abili ties of the opponent, the middle should be crowded, which will close off the area and force the offense to work the ball outside.

"Crowd the middle"

The cutting play is being used extensively by most teams and can be employed from any position.

If the offense overloads to the left, sending a cutter through as the ball is swung to the right, this may be handled by swinging the front line or pulling the center to the area involved. Either of these two moves will cover the offensive move just mentioned. (These movements are dis cussed in Chapter 3, Diagrams 15, 16 and 17.)

If these two moves cannot be made successively several strategic moves may be necessary in order to stop the cutter. The movement in the following two patterns is rather simple. They are not expressed to impose upon the proficiency of the coaching profession but to show the simple movement of the Match-Up in its earliest stages.

In the event a team employs two cutters in a pattern, which presents an opportunity to score on either side of the court, see Diagram 35 for the offensive movement and Diagram 36 for the match-up of this movement.

In case of two cutters through for an eventual scoring at tempt on the weak side of the court, a diagram is not neces sary because the cutters have been defensed individually in several of the diagrams in this chapter.

When a team employs the double cut through with an

eventual attempt to score on the weak side, the Match-Up defense has a choice of methods. Specifically, the double cut through leaves only three players left with the responsibility of getting the ball in position for the scoring attempt. This presents a defensive opportunity to either cut off the passing lanes by overplaying an area, trapping the

Diagram 20

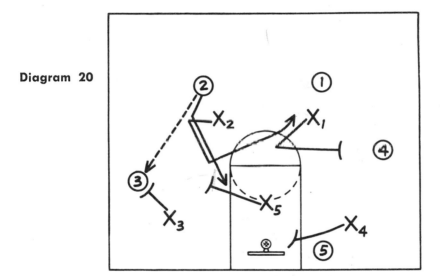

ball, and finally, of course, overplaying the cutters as demonstrated in this chapter. Time is available for these techniques since the ball must be passed around the perimeter; few teams are successful with the cross court pass and the Match-Up thrives on this type of move because of its overplay.

Without being too repetitious, most cutters, regardless of the number, can be handled by swinging the front line if the ball is allowed to be passed around the perimeter. Or, the middle position may be pulled to the corner when the cutters are allowed to form an overload.

METHOD

1. The cutter should always be crowded or over-played as much as possible.
2. When the ball is passed to (3), X4 and X5 sluff.
3. When (3) receives the ball, X3 plays an aggressive man-to-man situation.
4. As (2) cuts for the basket, X2 moves in front of him and follows until X5 zones the movement sufficiently.
5. X4 sluffs to help under the basket but is alert to pull back out on (4) if the ball is passed around the perimeter to his side.
6. X1 may cover (1), move back and zone (1) and (4), or try to steal the ball when it is passed to (1) from (3).

METHOD

1. X1 moves with (1) as he passes the ball to (2). If he is not needed to cover (1), he may help zone the middle.
2. X2 covers (2), who cuts to his right.

Diagram 21

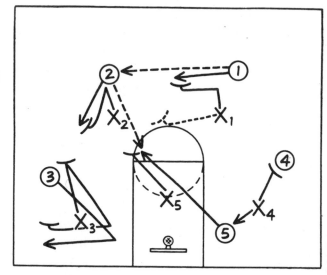

3. X3 plays between (3) and the ball. When (3) cuts for the basket X3 moves under the basket and eventually to the corner. X3 remains in a man-to-man situation.

4. X5 covers (5) aggressively. He may receive help from X1 and X2. The ball should be forced outside if possible.

5. X4 plays a zone defense. He sluffs under the basket for a rebound, covers (4), or helps out in the foul lane area.

SWITCHING ON THE HALF-COURT WEAVE

When the weave is employed against the Match-Up it is usually in the form of a stall game or a possession game. Sometimes either of these attacks will be used as an attempt to pull the defense outside. As a progressive step in teaching the Match-Up, the weave drill can be used to improve individual defense as well as to present situations that will occur with the other offensive patterns.

The three man weave does not provide many difficulties for the Match-Up unless a cutter is involved with the movement. In practice we defend against the five man, or figure eight continuity weave, which involves three defensive players in the vicinity of the ball and at the same time acquaints the other two defensive players with their position away from the ball.

Against the 3-2 offense, the weak side corner player must pull out. A situation such as this will arise many times during the regular season. Many problems that ordinarily come up when teaching the rules of the Match-Up will be solved by acquainting the squad with switching out front and overplay on the weak side.

Basically the switch situation in the Match-Up is the

same as the usual man-to-man technique. When a switch is made both defensive players step forward in order to play their new assignments tightly on the exchange. The front players never fight through a screen but stay relatively in the same area. This is different from the straight man-to-man defense in which the player on the ball usually tightens up and the player off the ball loosens up to let him through. A possible roll off a tight defense such as this is not a real scoring threat since the back line will handle the cutter with a converge. The switching tactic and converge on the cutter should be practiced until it becomes automatic.

The "blind pick" from the weave presents another problem that should become habitual with defensive practice. The Three-On-Three With a Screen Drill has already exposed the defensive maneuvers that are needed to combat a screen that takes effect from behind. With the Match-Up the defense may fight over the screen that takes place from behind and stay with the ball in most situations. When the pick is evident, a verbal warning should suffice since the situation has been practiced with previous drills.

If the weave is run on the outside without a cutter, the defense simply switches as the offense exchange positions.

It is wise to defense the weave at half speed early in the season, usually during the first few days of practice. At half speed the back line defense can develop converging and sluffing traits while the front line is putting pressure on the ball with the switch and other measures needed to stop the weave. It should be made clear to the corner players how to pull up high on the weak side and to the middle player how to help out in the corners. It also moves the front players from a position out front and acquaints them with the necessity of collapsing to the middle and later moving back out front for a new assignment.

METHOD

1. Arrange the squad into teams. If there are not enough players for three full teams, divide the squad equally into two groups and interchange players as desired. The third team can exchange with one of the teams when desirable.

2. Before the offense starts moving have the defense pull out on their relative assignments similar to a man-to-man defense.

3. X1 moves with (1) to the middle after he passes off and immediately moves out to cover (2) who has replaced (1).

4. X2 moves up with (2), playing him tightly since he has the ball, until X1 has moved back out to cover the ball. X2 then moves back to cover (5) who has moved up to replace (2).

5. X3 covers (5) at the start of the movement. He covers him loosely since he must eventually help cover the cutter, (1), who is coming to the middle and then to the corner.

6. X4 covers (3) aggressively since he is in a position to receive the ball. X4 is alert to sluff off and help

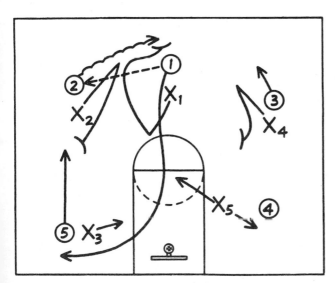

Diagram 22

around the foul lane area and to eventually move back to the corner if he is needed.

7. X5 must protect the middle against the cutter and be alert for a long pass to (4). X5 will probably be moving in and out of the foul lane area but should always be available to help stop the drive situation.

8. The complete movement should be run from both sides of the court.

TRAPPING THE WEAVE

To trap the weave have one of the front players move in front of the dribbler and have the opposite front player close in on him from behind, thus forming a trap. When the trap play is attempted other defensive players are alerted to close up the middle and the weak side corner player should be ready to pull out to a high position in order to fill in the space left by the front player trapping the ball.

METHOD

1. X2 moves in front of the ball as (2) dribbles to his right.

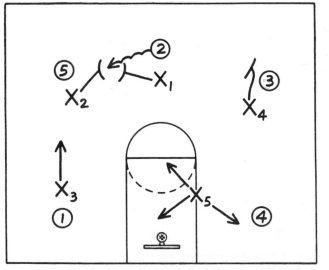

Diagram 23

2. X1 moves in behind (2) forming the trap.
3. X4 overplays (3). If he cannot get to the position in time for an overplay another trap could be formed by X1 and X4.
4. X5 sluffs to the side but should be alert to cover the middle area.
5. X3 overplays (1) in order to intercept a possible pass from (2).
6. The trap may be started from either of the front positions.

THE SCREEN AND ROLL

The screen and roll play is one of the most effective in basketball. It is used against many types of defense with outstanding success but the switching man to man is probably the least effective defense against this maneuver.

The play is usually performed by two players and can be executed at any combination of positions. It is more effective if the ball is involved with the two players who are working the play. It is also being used extensively by many teams as an effective out-of-bounds play which proves it has merit without directly involving the ball.

Two good attacking points for the screen and roll against the Match-Up are the front and corner positions.

When using the Match-Up to stop the roll, there will always be help nearby regardless of the position from which the play is attempted. Pressure must constantly be applied to the roller by moving with him aggressively. The most likely help will come from the middle position. The defensive corner position on the weak side must also be alert to help the middle. Most often he is the farthest away from the ball; therefore, the offense would have less opportunity to score an easy basket against the defensive over play.

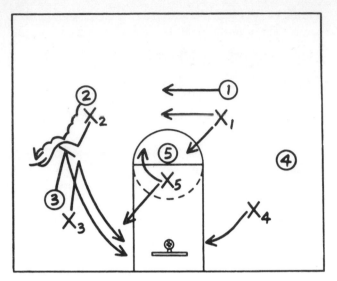

Diagram 24

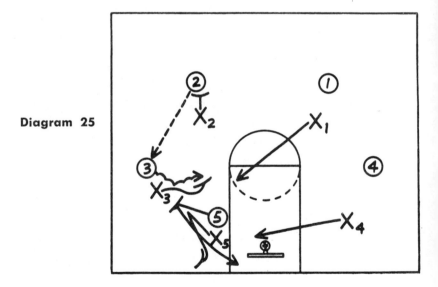

Diagram 25

Diagram 24 shows the defensive movement against the guard-forward screen and roll which attacks from the front of the defense. Diagram 25 shows the defensive movement against the center-forward screen and roll which attacks from the corner of the defense.

METHOD

1. X3 moves with (3). He is alert to talk with team-mate X2, warning him of the screen.

2. When (3) rolls off X2, X3 must be alert for a lead pass over his head. He can handicap the movement of (3) by playing him aggressively. The roller, (3), must be literally pushed or forced as he moves under the basket. The possibilities of a defensive foul are evident but remote. This maneuver can be handled aggressively without fouling.

3. If (3) does "beat" X3, then X5 may be in a position to help. X5 must zone (5) while (2) has the ball on the side.

4. X4 sluffs and rebounds, checking out (1).

5. X1 covers (1) or sluffs to the middle.

6. In this particular diagram the main scoring threat is the dribbler. It is evident that X2 may not successfully fight over the screen on every occasion. Note the roll-off player, (3) is virtually ineffective because of the zone tactics by X1 who sluffs to cover the middle area, by X5 who sluffs to cover (3) near the basket and by X3 who overplays (3) during his initial cut.

7. When X2 cannot fight over the screen X3 will take the dribbler which will make the medium jump-shot ineffective. X2 must attempt to play the cutter. Screen and roll exponents admit that the roll-out will not work unless a switch is made and this usually involves a man-to-man situation defense. But, remember the Match-Up reverts to zone strategy against man-to-man offense of this type. In this case X5 must aggressively assume the duty of neutralizing the cutter.

METHOD

1. X3 plays (3) aggressively trying to keep him from receiving the ball. When (3) receives the ball X3 tries to force him away from the screen. When the screen is set X3 works over the top to stay with (3) in order to handicap a pass or shot.

2. X5 plays (5) aggressively. When (5) rolls off, X5 rides him under the basket so he cannot receive a lead pass from (3).

3. X2 plays (2) aggressively trying to handicap his pass. If the pass is made X2 stays between (2) and (3) in order to cut off a return pass.

4. X4 sluffs under the basket. He may check (4) off the board or help out with (5).

5. X1 sluffs to the middle after the pass to the side.

6. Optional move: As mentioned previously the screen and roll is a man-to-man tactic, signaling once again the use of zone defensive principles. If X3 cannot fight over the screen X5 must now cover the dribbler aggressively forcing him to dribble high in order to give X1 an opportunity to help out. This means that X3 must overplay the cutter. He can receive help from X4 who has sluffed under the basket.

ONE-THREE-ONE OFFENSIVE PATTERNS

The one-three-one offense has been effective against the zone defense for many years. In order to save valuable time many teams will attack any type of defense from this formation. They will screen, drive, cut, and interchange players in much the same procedure regardless of the defense.

Many features of this offense put the Match-Up in a

favorable position. The one-on-one situation which is created certainly can be curtailed with sluffing maneuvers before the player with the ball reaches the vicinity of the goal or a good shooting area.

Spreading of the offensive wing men will allow the defense to form a double team situation or allow them to crowd areas of the floor that present a scoring threat. This is due, usually because the opposite wing man is out of contention and can be disregarded on occasion. These same wing men are out of rebound contention most of the time since they are such a distance from the basket.

Any time the ball is moved outside by the offense for readjustment purposes, the defense will have the same opportunity to adjust. If the defense has been over playing a maneuver, the opportunity to readjust is welcome.

Moving the offensive base-line performer back and forth along the end line may create a problem, especially when the defense is trying to adjust its rule situation. If the offense employs no cutting, the answer is simple. One of the corner positions can be assigned to guard the roamer on a man-to-man basis. He should play between the roamer and the ball. The remainder of the team can take their assignment according to the rules listed in Chapter 3 and disregard the player moving back and forth on the base-line.

Very seldom will an offense be this simple to defense. My teams have used the plan just mentioned. When the opponent has no continuity or cutting movement they have a tendency to start free lancing. Zone tactics of defense must be emphasized in order to bluff the opponent into staying in zone methods of offense, such as a straight 1-3-1 attack. Many times a team will judge the defense as a man-to-man when the match-up comes about and change their maneuvers accordingly. This is when the Match-Up is most effective.

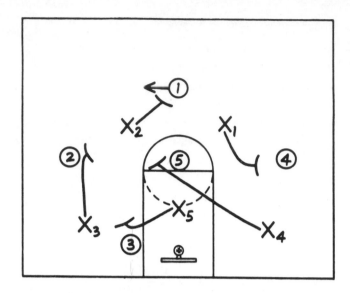

Diagram 26

METHOD

1. X5 covers the roamer, (3), man-to-man staying between him and the ball. He disregards the rule theory since it is assumed from the scouting report that no cutting will occur from the wing positions.

2. X4 moves to the middle and covers (5) with aggressive man-to-man play.

3. X1 sluffs to zone (4) if the ball is on the other side of the court. If the ball comes to his side of the court he will play (4) man-to-man.

4. X2 covers (1) aggressively. He may sluff to the middle if (1) is no threat from the outside.

5. X3 covers (2) aggressively when the ball is on his side. He may zone his area if the ball moves to the opposite side of the court.

6. Closing the gap and converging are important moves from this defensive set up. One-on-one situations will occur so zone tactics such as sluff-

ing and cutting off the area around the basket are important.

If liberties can be taken with the front line of the 1-3-1 offense then swinging the front line of the defense will match the play perfectly. If liberties may be taken with the offense on the base line or middle area then pulling the center to the corner will solve the offense. See both of these moves in the previous chapter.

Continuity from the 1-3-1 presents some problems for the Match-Up. As the ball is brought across mid-court the front line of the Match-Up should glance over their shoulder and see which side of the court the roamer or player under the basket is located. The ball should be forced to this side of the court so the rules may start from the side in which the base-line player is located. As soon as the offense is matched by this method the offense will most likely start their continuity.

The following three continuity patterns from the 1-3-1 may give the reader an insight concerning the general movement of the Match-Up with most threats from this type of offense.

Diagram 27

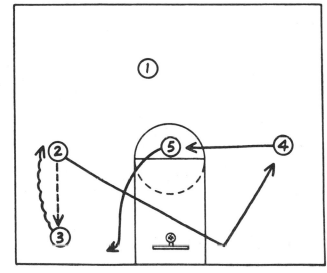

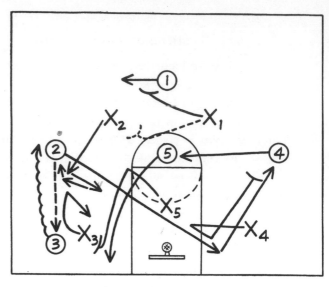

Diagram 28

METHOD

1. X1 covers (1). He has the option of sluffing off and crowding the middle if (1) is not an outside threat.

2. X2 covers (2) as the ball is passed to the side. Since (2) is the second player from the base-line he must be covered until he is released to the middle area. After releasing him X2 moves to the side to cover (3), who is coming up from the base-line.

3. X3 plays (3) aggressively on the base-line, stopping the drive if it is attempted. As soon as (3) starts his dribble up the side, X3 moves back to help cover (5), who has moved to the base-line. By this time X2 has covered (3). It must be kept in mind that the primary job of X3, against this particular cutting series, is to protect the base-line area.

4. X5 plays a zone defense on the side of the foul lane and helps cover (2) as he moves through the area. (5) must also be zoned by X5 as he moves

from the foul line to the base-line. If (3) is not an outside shooter, X3 can help stop up the middle.

5. X4 sluffs under the basket to rebound if a quick shot is taken. He also covers (2) as he comes through the back side of the foul lane area. In order to have good rebound position and be in a position to cover the next cutter he must play between (2) and the ball. If the ball is allowed to be passed around the perimeter to this side of the court X4 would of course have to play an aggressive man-to-man situation.

METHOD

1. After the ball has been passed to the side X1 sluffs to the middle area and then moves out to cover (5) if needed.
2. X2 covers (2) aggressively.
3. X3 plays (3), making it as difficult as possible for him to receive a pass. As (3) cuts across the base-line area he is released to the zoning tactics of X5. X3 then moves out to pick up (1) who is cutting between the side line and the middle area to the corner.

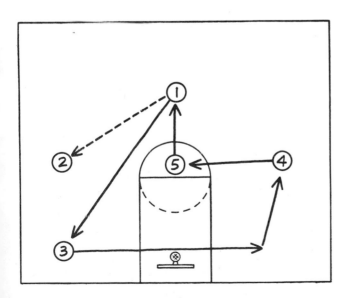

Diagram 29

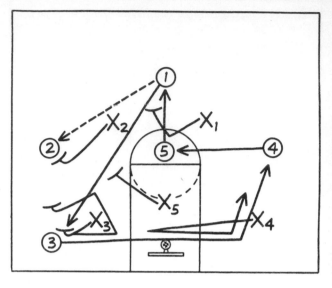

Diagram 30

4. X5 zones the middle area playing high in front of (3) as he passes through under the basket. He must be in a position to help with (1) as he passes through. Once the offense has set in the 1-3-1 again, X5 will zone the middle area probably protecting against (4) who has moved to that area.

5. X4 sluffs under the basket to cover (3) and possibly to rebound if a quick shot is taken. He covers (3) closely if the ball is allowed to be passed around to that side of the court.

METHOD

1. X1 may cover (1) if needed. He has the option to sluff to the middle area and help cover (5) and/or pull out on (2) who is moving out to replace (1).

2. X2 covers (2) upon the pass and then overplays (1) on the guard around play. He releases (1) to X5 in the middle and pulls back out to cover (3) who is moving up to replace (2).

3. X3 covers (3) in the corner by playing in front of him so he cannot receive a pass from (2). If he does get the ball and dribbles up the side as

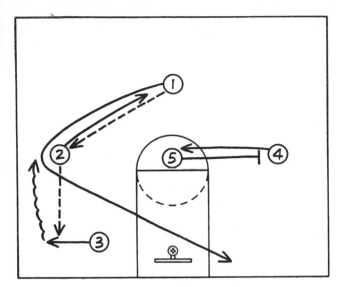

Diagram 31

Diagram 32

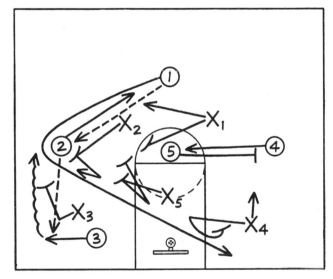

indicated he guards him aggressively until he is released to X2.

4. X5 zones the middle area covering (1) as he passes through and also may zone (5) and (4) on the foul line but will receive help from X1 more than likely.

5. X4 sluffs under the basket picking up (1) and gets rebound position if a shot is taken.

THE LOW POST

The low post is a popular location mainly because most tall men can score with very little effort from this area.

Very few college teams operate without the exceptionally tall pivot man. Placing him in the low post position greatly helps a team's rebounding. The deceptive passing, dribbling, and ball handling exhibited in today's game will clear him for easy baskets. The ability of the forwards to score from the corners also helps this attack. It tends to pull the defense out, thus opening the middle and giving the post man room to move. Many teams use a screen to free the low post man and this is done in a number of ways. These situations are listed in order to point out the offensive effects that must be covered.

Most shots in basketball are taken from the foul lane area and the Match-Up is geared to concentrate on the area by sluffing and employing some zone tactics. The weak side front position and the weak side corner position are the key players when double teaming or sluffing to cover the effective pivot player who locates around the basket.

METHOD

1. X1 covers (1). He has an alternative to move into the middle if (1) is not a scoring threat.
2. X2 covers (2), the dribbler; he moves to the side and plays him aggressively. X2 tries to deflect or handicap (2)'s pass to (4) in the corner.
3. X3 covers (3) and covers him to the foul lane area. He then moves to the base-line to cover (4), who has moved away from X5.
4. X5 zones the middle, protecting against (4), momentarily, and later (5), who is moving from the low post.

5. X4 plays in front of (4) as he comes around the corner and across under the basket and then picks up (3) coming through the foul lane.

TWO-THREE CONTINUITIES

When matching an offense that involves a continuity there are two threats that must be covered—the movement

Diagram 33

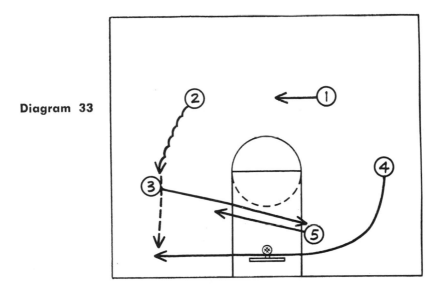

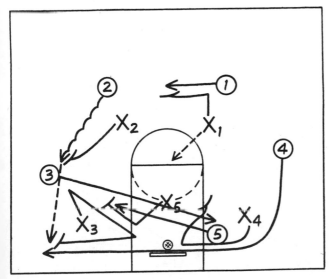

Diagram 34

of the ball when it is reversed to the weak side and the cutters. From a two-three formation these two moves are very effective against the zone and require special attention.

An outstanding feature of this offense is the movement of the ball to the opposite side of the court from which the play started. Trapping is made difficult by spreading the offense while the cutters locate in good scoring areas. When the ball is eventually moved to the weak side area,

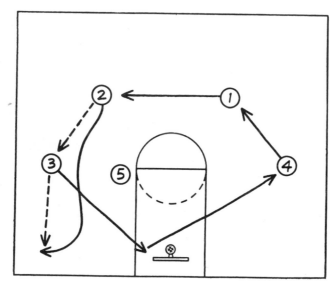

Diagram 35

Diagram 36

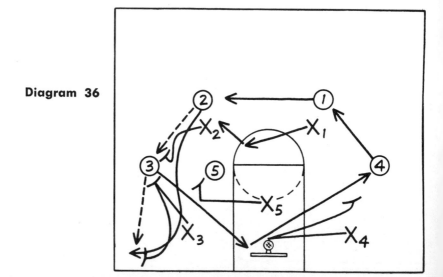

the offense on this side must be covered man-to-man in order to stop the open set shot, the jump shot, or the drive situation that may arise.

Many teams move the ball to the strong side as a decoy and then move the ball from side to side several times times with an exchange of positions. The offense hopes for an eventual defensive assignment to be missed or that the movement will be covered haphazardly after several cutting plays have been made. In this instance the Match-Up must employ talk, sliding and sluffing tactics along with other signals in order to constantly cover the movement.

METHOD

1. X2 sluffs to the area of (3) as (2) cuts through to the corner. (2) should be overplayed as he moves by the ball.

2. X3 releases (3) and takes up (2), who has now become the first player from the base-line. (NOTE: The ideal defensive move would be to pull the middle position to the corner but adjustment on the weak side would be handicapped. It is important to keep the middle position near the basket with this type of play. At this point, X2 plays (3) aggressively and X3 and X5 may cover as he cuts to the foul lane area.)

3. X5 plays a zone defense. He protects the middle against both cutters, (2) and (3) X2 releases (3) and moves back out front to cover (1). While moving from (3) to (1) X2 may also protect against (5) with a sluffing movement.

4. As the ball goes to the opposite corner, X4 moves under the basket to rebound or cover (3) who was released by X5 when he moved out of the scoring area.

Diagram 37

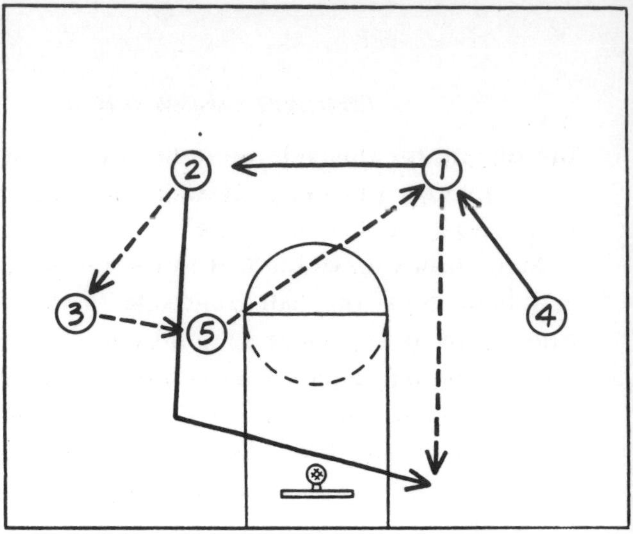

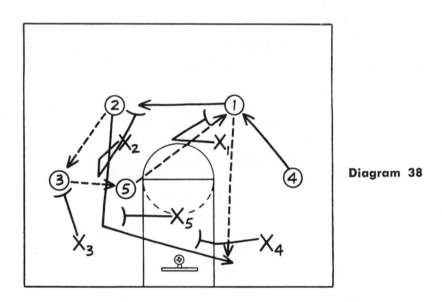

Diagram 38

5. When (1) moved to replace (2), X1 zoned the area until X2 moved back into position. X1 then moved over to cover (4), who has moved outside on the continuity.

METHOD

1. When (2) passes to (3) and cuts, X2 covers him to the foul lane area. As X2 releases (2) to X5

he helps protect against (5) from the front. As soon as (2) has left the area from which he could receive the ball other adjustments may start.

2. X2 now moves out front to cover (1), who has moved over to replace (2). If X2 is not needed out front, he sluffs to the middle area.

3. X1 sluffs to the middle as the ball is passed to (3). He then moves out to cover (4) who is in a position to receive the ball. (NOTE: If liberties may be taken with the outside players, (3) and (1) could swing the front line which would be the ideal move.)

4. X4 sluffs under the basket to rebound and/or cover (2) as X5 releases him.

5. X3 covers (3) aggressively, cutting off his passing lanes if possible.

5

MATCHING
SPECIAL SITUATIONS

When the need arises, offense is usually ready with the special play. Consequently, the defense must be prepared to meet these situations. Thus, defensing the jump ball, the free throw, the out-of-bounds play—both from under the basket and from the sideline—should be thoroughly learned. Defense of this type is not often overlooked but many times a team will not put enough emphasis on this phase of the game. If a definite scheme of defense is not presented and practiced, a passive attitude could develop when these situations are faced at critical times during a game. A team well versed in the aspects of defensing the special play will win more than its share of the close games.

DEFENSING THE OUT-OF-BOUNDS PLAY

Defensing the out-of-bounds play in the front court is an integral part of team defense. During a game, the opportunity to score from the side and under the basket comes about several times and pattern play from these locations is popular for several reasons. The official must handle the ball which gives the offense time to set up a particular formation. Time is available for the offense to call certain plays and to change them before movement starts if the defense has adjusted. The transition on the part of each individual defensive player from regular offense facing mid-court to facing the basket on out-of-bounds play requires good mental and physical adjustment. Defense is usually standing still when the out-of-bounds play starts, which is an unfavorable defensive situation. This helps emphasize the fact that alert defense in this instance is a necessity.

Always defend the out-of-bounds play

During the semi-finals of the Florida Class AA State Tournament in 1959, Hillsborough High was playing Miami High. With less than four minutes left to play the score was tied and Hillsborough called time out since they had possession. The referee had the ball at mid-court signifying the area from which the teams would resume play. When Hillsborough came out they intentionally set up on Miami's end of the court, facing Miami High's basket. The complete Miami team erroneously placed themselves between their own basket and the Hillsborough players. In other words, Hillsborough had no defense between them and their own basket. Hillsborough quickly took advantage of the situation and scored a wide open lay-up. Miami High seemed befuddled from their mental error and eventually lost the game as Hillsborough scored 17 points in less than four minutes.

In 1962, Hillsborough attempted the same play under similar circumstances during the State tournament. The play failed this time because the defense did not have the mental lapse that had made it so effective three years earlier. An out-of-bounds play of this type does not work very often especially against teams that play sound defense as Miami High has done for years. The example serves to emphasize how important it is to defense the out-of-bounds play regardless of the area in which it originates.

Psychology is involved

The predominantly offensive-minded coach intimates that special plays may mean the difference between losing and winning the game. He also asserts that when a special play scores or wins a game the psychological effect has terrific impact because the confidence derived means future victories. At the same time he implies that plays from out-of-bounds anywhere on the court make a team look well coached. I agree wholeheartedly. However, why wouldn't good defense against these special plays serve the same purpose? Usually the average fan doesn't recognize a defensive play that is effective because the team is working as a group. Response to team effort is not admired in comparison with the action of a scoring effort. Unless an individual blocks a shot or steals a pass, good defensive play goes unnoticed most of the time. If one or two field goals from a special set-up will win a game, then defensing these attempts successfully will win games. My teams have taken great pride in stopping the scoring attempt from out-of-bounds with a very simple approach.

Unnecessary to match-up every play

It would almost be impossible to match-up every out-of-bounds formation simply because the time involved would not be rewarding enough just to work against plays that will be faced only two or three times a game. The opponent already has the ball and a steal from the side or under the basket is difficult to achieve. Why not permit them to throw the ball outside of the scoring area and attack them from a familiar formation where the basic defense will be employed? In order to prove this theory the offensive formation, the type of play undertaken, and the area from which the play is attempted must be discussed.

Many teams are not satisfied with just putting the ball back in play; they want to score. They want to keep you guessing by using different formations and signals. Verbal numbers, hand signals, and the location of the ball at a predetermined time during the play are some of the methods used to signify which option will be emphasized. All of these methods are based on the idea of taking advantage of best player abilities, placing rebound strength near the basket when the shot is taken, and using counter plays or options when the main threat is stopped. These statements make it evident that trying to stop all the minute phases of out-of-bounds play would be perplexing if each point had to be defensed individually.

Let them set-up. Then match -up

What is the answer? It's so simple that at first glance it may be deceiving. *Invite the opponent to pass the ball out of immediate scoring range and then move into the regular rules of the Match-Up.* The opponent already has possession in a location that is unfamiliar to rule defense, so you would not be giving them anything by encouraging a pass to an area that can be attacked with regular defense. It is not impossible to employ the regular rules of defense against the out-of-bounds play, but valuable practice time would be consumed preparing for the various moves.

Against the out-of-bounds play the Match-Up employs a unison movement similar to the zone defense in order to keep the offense away from the high percentage shot. At this point the reader may be thinking he has learned nothing from this seemingly common theory. The proof of effective defense is not in the formation or general idea of a theory but in team and individual position.

The unison movement of the zone against this play assures the defense that the area around the basket is protected, that the screen and roll play is ineffective in the middle area, and that good rebound position is certain if the outside shot is taken.

Get close to the basket

The 2-3 formation should be set up as close to the basket as possible in the area of the ball. An attempt should be made to cover as much floor space as possible with each player extending his arms and taking up as much area as practicable. Since no attempt is being made to steal the ball on the first pass, little attention should be given the point of the ball. Care must be taken under the basket so the offense cannot get a set position in a scoring area near the basket. When defensing a play that originates from under the basket, set the three players on the base-line area far enough under the hoop in order to force offensive set ups to line up or move to areas where shooting is prohibitive and rebounding contention is at a minimum. Passing the ball back to mid-court is encouraged by purposely leaving the outside area open and closing the area around the top of the circle.

During my first years of coaching my teams played a strict man-to-man defense except when the opponent had

the ball out-of-bounds under the basket or at the side
near the basket. When these situations came about we
playcd a 2-3 zone defense and stayed in this formation
until the ball exchanged hands. The next time down
court we would be back in our man-to-man defense.
Changing defense in this manner was easy to coordinate
and seemed to confuse the opposition. Even though the
Match-Up is my basic defense today the zone theory seems
to confuse the offense on the out-of-bounds play.

Playing the out-of-bounds play with the zone theory
assures the coach that he must prepare only for the zone
type of play. The basket is protected until the ball is
moved into an area that allows the regular defense to
form.

Zone "jam" areas

The areas of attack by the offense against the zone that
"jams" the area near the basket are the top of the circle and
the corners. Consequently, plays are usually designed for
the best outside shooter.

If the two outside players on the zone line up tight
around the foul line, a play may be designed to screen
these players. For instance, the four offensive players inbounds line up along the outside of the defense in order
to keep them from breaking through to stop the shooter.
A block-out here is imminent. The shooter moves from
the line to behind the line to receive the pass and attempts a shot over the block.

The best method to combat this type of play is to
mcve the outside line of defense farther out which makes
the pass inbounds time consuming and the area from
which the shot must be taken farther from the basket
than is desirable. Care must be taken not to leave the
middle area of the defense open. The big strong boys

are usually designated as the blockers and if the first option does not work, a cut to the middle area by one of these players could cause trouble if caution is not taken.

The defensive players on the base-line will have their arms extended but a special effort should be put forth to force the ball to the outside area. If the ball is successfully passed inside the defense, a converge on the ball would suffice since the defense is in tight enough to make it effective. Placing one of the outside players behind the blocking line may be effective but this move leaves open area on either side of the circle. When placing one of the front players behind the blocking line, alert the corner defensive players to help out from a high position on their side of the court.

If the ball is passed to a deep corner position the defense should move in unison, closing the area to the basket until the ball is passed outside.

Defending a screen from the weak side

A good out-of-bounds play against any type of defense is a screen from the weak side. This type of play has probably been employed more than any against the zone from out-of-bounds. The ball is usually passed high to the side area. The desired effect is to have the defense follow the ball with eyes and body movement. A screen is set on the weak side by a player or players who originally set up in the area. As the ball is passed around the perimeter a screen is placed on the weak side corner. The player who passed the ball inbounds has timed his move to receive a pass and take a shot over the screen. The best method used to stop this play is to cut off the passing lanes when an attempt is made to get the ball around the perimeter of the defense. If liberties cannot be taken with this move, the corner position will have to fight over the screen to cover the prospective shooter. The latter should not be difficult because reaction time is available while the ball is being worked around the perimeter.

DEVELOPING DOWN COURT DEFENSE

An obvious need for down court defense is to stop the fast break, and the most effective place to stop the fast break is on the backboard, but this cannot always be done. Stopping the outlet pass is another place to stop the quick break; however, these two methods of defense are primarily individual efforts. An accurate changeover from offense to defense is important. The changeover must be broken down into various categories in order to get the full effect of good team defense.

Individual effort is paramount. Initially, the Match-Up offers no patented technique. However, once the full squad has arrived at the defensive basket, basic rules go into effect and there are some precautions that are considered normal individual defensive tactics that must be taken into consideration.

The one-on-one drill will help develop most individual defensive abilities but the two-on-one, the three-on-one, the three-on-two, the two-on-two and the change from these situations to team theory must be coordinated.

Following is a discussion of these methods which involves some general theory on how to defense these offensive threats.

Tandem. The tandem defense locates in front of the basket to stop the fast break. This defense necessitates two players getting down court before a scoring attempt is made.

The first player down court locates just in front of the basket to protect against the lay-up. The second player down court places himself at the foul line. Both of these players spread their arms and cover as much floor space as possible. The front player's responsibility is to put pressure on the dribbler, consequently slowing him down or making his attempted pass as ineffective as possible. When a pass is made to one of the wing men moving toward the basket, the player located under the basket moves out to cover him. The defensive player on the foul line will drop back opposite the pass ready to defense a possible pass from the wing. If the ball moves back out to the foul line the same defensive tandem is formed. If a pass is allowed cross court the defensive player originally located on the foul line covers the receiver, who will probably be under the basket. The defensive player who was originally under the basket must now move out to a position to cover the offensive player on the foul line and the wing man opposite the ball.

If a team is hustling back on defense the complete unit will be located around the area of the basket by the time the first pass is made. If the defense is caught short they surely will be down court by the time the second pass is made.

Two-Man Zone. The two-man zone is effective when the ball handler cannot shoot from the foul line. This would be determined by the scouting report. The defensive players locate themselves midway and on either side of the free throw lane but do not pressure the ball

They station themselves with good body position and zone the ball until some help arrives. With the two-man zone, care must be taken not to leave the area in front of the basket open. The defense should attempt to cut off passing lanes and force the fast breaking team to hurry their passes and shots.

At the same time you may be willing to give the opponent the long jump shot in order to completely stop the lay-up.

The Two-on-One or Three-on-One Situation. When the offensive team gains a two-on-one or a three-on-one advantage the procedure is different because the defensive player is by himself. The first objective is to protect the basket and not give the opponent the easy lay-up. Fakes, feints, and arm and body movement should be employed to force the offense to slow up the ball or hurry their shot. Let's face it, the defense is in a desperate situation. Stop the drive, but never pull out and leave the immediate area of the basket unguarded. A hurried shot from ten, twelve, or fifteen feet is much less effective than a lay-up attempt. The defensive player should fake and feint toward the ball, gradually dropping back in front of the basket—maybe help will arrive.

Stopping the Trailer. Many times a defensive team will recover quickly enough to match the offensive attack with equal numbers only to have a trailer break through for an easy basket.

The middle player handing the ball will probably veer to one side of the foul line in order to give the trailer room to move through. If the trailer is ahead of the remaining defensive players the foul lane area should be closed off by the players already located on defense.

I have always instructed my teams to get back on defense as quickly as possible but to come down the middle of the court. The short-cut theory is once again put into effect by moving down the middle of the court and the opponent can be curtailed more effectively since most fast breaking teams bring the ball down in this area.

Getting back on defense cannot be done effectively unless it is practiced. Scrambling to get located for team defense has allowed many cheap baskets. This inadvertently happens with younger boys if it is not developed cautiously.

A drill that will help develop the quick change from offensive to defense is the Changeover Drill.

Team A works its offensive pattern while team B is playing half court defense. The coach or manager stands under the basket with another ball and rolls or throws it on the court at any time. Team B picks up the ball that is thrown on the court and fast breaks or hurries down court to attempt a quick shot. Team A drops its offensive attack and gets back on defense as quickly as possible moving down the middle of the court. Once down court the defense must get good defensive floor and body position around the immediate area of the basket.

Many times the smaller players are the first back on defense. This means they must eventually move outside to locate for their half court defensive assignment. When the defensive players, who are stationed under the basket, arrive to take up their duties, the exchange of positions must be done carefully but quickly. Talk is important. An offensive threat must be consciously released so that other defensive players at hand are aware of what is happening. Then, the half court defense is gradually formed as the offense locates to set up their regular attack.

MATCHING-UP OR DEFENSING THE JUMP BALL

Depending upon the type of defense that is advocated the number of jump ball situations in a game will vary. Generally, a game will average about 15 jumps. It is imperative that a team have in its scheme something for combating the jump ball from a defensive or cover situation when at a physical (height, speed, jumping ability, etc.) disadvantage. Needless to say, dominating the jump by getting possession will increase the total points or increase the number of times the opponent will have to play your type of game. Never will a team have the advantage in every jump situation so it's important that some type of possession game be planned rather than free lance aggressiveness on an individual basis.

Key the jump

One of the most important factors involved with the jump ball is getting the proper formation lined up. Time is usually limited. Therefore, a code is needed in order to expedite the type of play and to locate the players. The jumper is the key to the play. He can call a prearranged number while the officials are getting the ball ready. In most instances the players will anticipate the type of jump to be used by comparing the size and abilities of his teammate with the opponent as the ball is tied up. The jumper should never step to the line until he has carefully checked to see that his teammates are in position.

Verbal signal best

For this type of play the verbal signal seems to be the most practical rather than holding up fingers or using some other gesture. A verbal type of signal can be given immediately and a teammate can locate himself without looking for the jumper. Various methods may be employed to code the play depending upon how many types of jump ball situations a team intends to employ. Usually a team will include a defensive jump in which possession is not the main purpose, an offensive jump when they are assured of possession, and a cover situation in which the team goes after the ball aggressively. A simple code would be to have the defensive formation end with the numeral 0, the offensive formation end with the numeral 2, the cover right formation end with the numeral 5, and the cover left formation end with the numeral 6. Any prefix before these numbers would only act as a decoy. (If the jumper yelled 45, the team would line up in a cover right formation. At the same time he could have yelled 25, 35, 55, etc. and call the same play.)

The defensive jump may be necessary at a time when the opponent is getting shots at the basket before team defense can be formulated or when the opponent has an outstanding advantage under their basket.

I have seen teams go so far as to purposely step in the circle causing a violation which gives the opponent the ball out-of-bounds as soon as contact is made with the ball. This move is difficult to understand. If a team is giving the ball away because they are at a height disadvantage, why couldn't some aggressiveness be guided toward the area of the tap? Regardless of the difference in the size of the two jumpers the ball may be played aggressively without taking too much of a chance.

Only 20 minutes/week coaching time

At this point most coaches are probably wondering how much time each week should be devoted to the jump ball situation. Once the fundamentals of the jump and tap have been mastered, twenty minutes a week will get the job done. Most of this time will be involved with going over opponents' plays from the scouting report.

The offensive jump formation may vary from the defensive jump or a cover play, but if every play can be coordinated from the same general set up, less learning and time will be involved. Offensive jump plays are explained in Chapter 6 which involves the fast break.

Suggestions for the receiver

Regardless of the type of jump being employed, there

are some points that the receiver should emphasize. It is a good idea to take up as much room around the circle as possible. It is not imperative that the defensive team get possession on the first tap although this is the intended goal. Many times just a finger or partial contact will present opportunities in which possession may be achieved. If possession is not acquired from a move such as this the play of the opponent will, in all probability, be handicapped. Each player should have his arms comfortably spread with his eye on the ball at all times. I like to see the prospective receivers practically hanging over the circle, poised with eyes on the ball, ready to spring into action regardless of the type of jump being employed.

The official is important to a successful jump play. Does he throw the ball high? Does he throw the ball quickly? Does he throw the ball with one hand or two hands? Does he allow room to move into the opponent on the jump? How much time does he allow to line up? These are questions that may help a team take some timely advantages if answered properly.

DEFENSIVE JUMP FORMATION

Following is the Defensive Jump Formation that my teams have used during recent years. It is closely coordinated with other jump situations. With little adjustment we can move into the cover jump to go after the ball or into one of our offensive plays when we are assured of the tap. With the 1-2-1-1 formation we are assured of a fair chance of getting the ball and at the same time we can get our players back into their half-court defensive formation without giving away a quick short shot when the opponent employs the fast break. In other words the defensive jump formation can do away with scrambling for position when half-court defense is important.

If the opponent taps forward we are in an excellent position to tap in the same direction and move the ball deep in the back court. The idea behind the tap in this instance is to not allow the opponent to place a soft tap to the spot he desires. At the same time the basic team defense is practically located. If the ball is successfully tapped deep in the back court the opponent can be easily screened out of the area allowing plenty of time to recover.

The play can be used at any of the circles when it is important to get back on defense rather than go after the ball.

Diagram 39

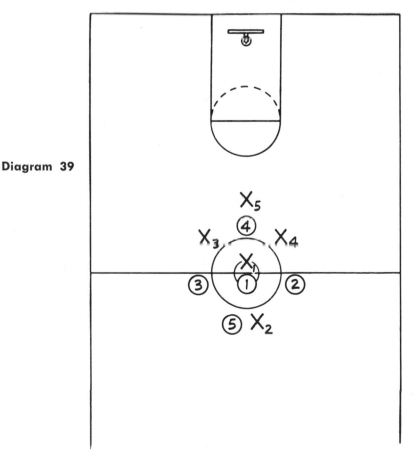

METHOD

1. X3, X4, and X5 should be the players that locate under the basket during regular defense. If the ball is tapped in this area they will have an opportunity to move after it and still get back on defense.

2. X1 does not necessarily have to be the best jumper but aggressiveness and size at this location are helpful.

3. X2 probably should be the weakest defensive player since he is located in the most expendable position. Naturally, if the ball is tapped or deflected to this area he plays for possession.

THE COVER JUMP PLAY

The Cover Jump Ball Play indicates exactly what the name implies. The area around the circle must be occupied by movement and the defensive basket protected at the same time. There is a certain amount of concealment but not necessarily by the placement of players around the circle. Concealment comes from the direction in which the players move. When the code, suggested earlier in the chapter, is employed and a number ending in 6 is indicated by the jumper, the team would move generally in the direction to their right after the ball. If a number ending in 5 is indicated by the jumper, the team would move in a direction to their left around the circle after the ball.

METHOD

1. X3 moves to his right covering the area between himself and X4.

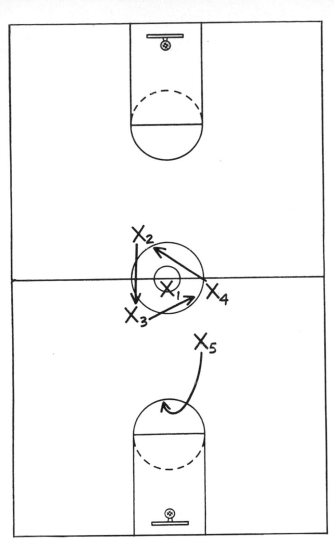

Diagram 40

2. X4 moves to his right covering the area between himself and X2.

3. X2 moves to his right covering the area between himself and X3.

4. X5 stays in fairly tight but ready to move back on defense under the basket if needed.

5. X1 is the jumper and taps to the area of X4 if the tap is controlled because this is the best area for the ball to be tapped if the jumper is right-handed.

ONE-THREE-ONE DEFENSIVE JUMP

Another jump pattern that is very popular which allows good opportunities to go after the ball is the 1-3-1 when employed for defensive purposes. This formation is demonstrated in Chapter 6 involving the fast break. The fact that the opposition is challenged at every area around the circle makes it very popular.

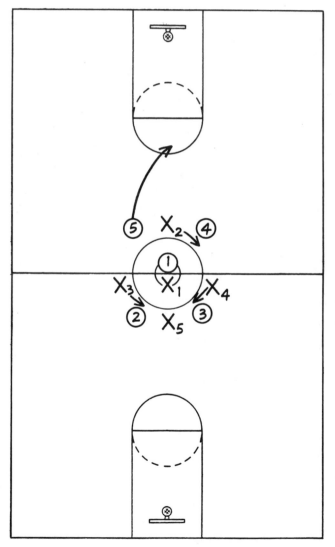

Diagram 41

METHOD

1. As the ball is tossed by the official, the two side men, X3 and X4 will cut in front of (2) and (3). They must be careful not to enter the circle until the tap is made.

2. X2 may cut in front of (4) or (5) if the ball is tapped back by (1).

3. X5 will drop back at the toss for a possible long tap and also for defensive measures.

4. All cutters will be moving toward the opponent's goal if possession is not acquired.

MATCHING-UP THE FREE THROW

A primary concern of the coach is a system whereby he will be able to defend adequately in free throw situations when his team is at the line. The following information offers some suggestions which are probably general knowledge to many. The coach can organize these procedures with his attack by deleting or adding other ideas. The team shooting a free throw should always match the opponent either with a man-to-man theory, a zone theory or a combination of the two, but one approach should be selected and coordinated in the same manner as the primary team defense is organized.

In Chapter 3, the stress on matching-up against the regular offenses depended upon the floor area, individual abilities from a particular area, and more or less, player stature which involves strength, agility, and size. Matching-up from the free throw cannot use all of these features since the formations employed by the opposing teams are usually irregular. Opposition will usually present so many variations that it is much easier to match them man-to-man and incorporate some zone practices when the opportunity arises.

The fundamental problem is getting the players quickly back into their normal half-court defensive alignment. There are several considerations to be kept in mind during this procedure. Then, too, a coach may desire to alter this normal procedure in favor of a more aggressive maneuver which involves an attempt to regain possession like the full-court press or half-court trap.

However, the coach is aware that there is more to defensing the free throw than just getting back.

Over the years there have been some unusual formations employed from the free throw, but probably the most prolific threat has been the fast break. During the past couple of years the break from this play has been less evident because defense and rebounding has improved. The decline has not diminished to the point that a team can forget about defensing this type of play.

If the attempt to stop the break from the foul shot is focused on putting two men under the defensive basket, then defensive work must be guided toward a tandem by these two players, toward zoning the area, or toward playing a man-to-man around the basket until the complete team arrives for the regular half-court defense.

If the defense decides to challenge the outlet pass to the side, the match-up probably will be involved on a man-to-man basis which may allow opportunities for double teaming or a combination of zone tactics.

Most teams like to stay as close to their regular defense as possible when combating the special play, but I contend that the ideal situation for something different is evident. A surprise element is easily keyed from this formation which, in all probability, will force the opposition to do something different. A made or missed free throw presents an ideal situation for the full-court, the three-quarter court, or the half-court trap. If a team has been running a zone defense, a change on this one play to a man-to-man defense may bring about a turnover play.

The following description of the duties of the shooter and rebounders suggest that aggressive individual attempts to regain possession, after the shot is taken, are all part of the over-all team defensive theory in the free throw situation.

The shooter

The free throw shooter is in position to carry out several defensive duties. His first function is to momentarily stay in position for a tap-out if the shot is missed. A field goal attempt from the foul line is a very high percentage shot but most teams will cover the shooter. Many times the long rebound will bounce to this area. The scouting report will indicate whether or not the tap-out should be attempted. The team can be conditioned for the play during the scouting report talk or during pre-game practice. Anytime the opponent crashes the board with all the personnel on the foul lane the tap naturally will be exploited.

The shooter is in a good position to steal an outlet pass, to move down court for team defense, to move down court to take part in the tandem, or to locate in a position for the trap press.

The best approach to defensing the players not on the foul lane is to keep it simple. Since we are emphasizing the Match-Up theory, the obvious answer is to match their formation. If they place two players on either side of the foul lane area, two defensive players should be placed between them and the basket in a position that will not allow the opponent to play his pattern. If the opponent places the complete team on the foul lane, the defensive team could make the same move but they should be careful to have enough players in position to get down court if needed. If the opponent places one player at the side of the free throw lane for the outlet pass or other reasons, one defensive player should be designated to stop the play.

A different approach may be taken when the opponent places players on the opposite end of the court. The man-to-man Match-Up theory from this area may achieve the desired effect but the tandem, or other methods, can be employed. The final word on defensing a situation like this will, of course, be determined by the over-all system to be developed.

The rebound

Rebounding may not necessarily be considered a part of defense, in the strict sense, but the following theory is a vital part of the total defensive picture.

The fact that the opposition has the inside area on the lane is no positive assurance that they will get possession. Some teams fail to do a strong job of screening-out from this area because it is evident they have an advantage and often will not pay much attention to the opponent. If I were to say that the strongest rebounders should be placed in the middle slots, I'm sure that nothing new would be presented. However, just placing them in that location is not the answer. Aggressive use of strength and agility could solve the problem and should be stressed regardless of the back court defense which comes about if the ball is not retrieved.

If you are over-matched so greatly that it would be almost impossible to get the ball over these inside players then another approach must be taken. If you can't go over them then go around them. Very seldom will a player in the middle be able to move from this position on the lane to an area under the basket by the time the ball comes off the board. However, many times he can get a good location on the side of his opponent which will allow him to steal the ball or tie it up. When employing this theory it is a good idea to send only one player after the ball. The player on the left side should go to the middle of the foul lane, attempting to get between the opposition. Since most rebounds come off the board on the right side, the player in the right lane should be designated to move about for the steal.[1]

METHOD

1. (1) moves around and to the inside of X1. He cannot enter the free throw lane before the ball touches the rim but he can be moving around X1 while the ball is in flight.

Diagram 42

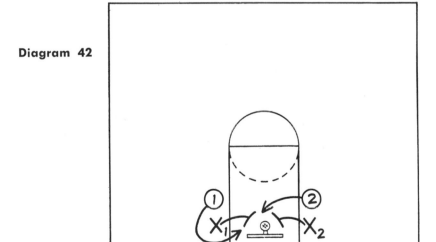

[1] Garland F. Pinholster, COACH'S GUIDE TO MODERN BASKET-BALL DEFENSE (Englewood Cliffs, N.J.: Prentice-Hall, Inc., 1961), p. 239.

2. (2) forces himself between X2 and X1 who are screening out the middle of the lane. Careful attention must be given to the area in which the rebound comes off.

OBTAINING THE BALL

We have just discussed various methods of defensing the opponent after a free throw, but there are some general ideas worthy of discussion which involve the team not shooting the free throw.

Cover the shooter

The shooter must be covered. It is not necessary that our scouts check our future opponents to see if they tap-out on a missed free throw. Most teams tap back to their shooter regardless of the defensive location and this presents an excellent opportunity to steal the ball. Regardless of whether the offense taps to the shooter, a player should be designated to move into the area to block-out and play for the ball from the tap-out or in case of an ordinary rebound.

If the offensive team places two players on one side of the foul lane (See Diagram 43), it is best for the player covering the shooter to move out near the foul line so that he will not get screened out. The rule states that every other area on the lane must be available to the opponent if they desire to occupy the location. When the area is not occupied by the opponent then the area may be filled by any player. With some moving around and adjusting, the foul line can be covered regardless of the location of the opponent. In fact, the player assigned to cover the shooter can screen out the player directly across the lane from him and still cover the foul line.

METHOD

>   1. X3 moves across the foul lane to cover (4) for
>   a possible tap-out on a missed foul shot. If (3) is
>   moving in the area and is in contention for the
>   rebound or tap-out, X3 blocks him out at the
>   same time he covers (4).

Blocking out from inside

Regardless of the over-all theory behind the approach
to stop the offense, proper alignment of personnel is important. Some factors that may seem like "old stuff" should
be taken into consideration.

Blocking out from the inside lanes would require reiteration of rebound methods discussed in Chapter 2. The
important point here is to keep the opponents outside
and not let them in between these two players. The forward pivot and eventual block-out is still in order regardless of the attempt made by the opposition to get the ball.
The 12-inch neutral zone allows room for maneuvering
which should be capitalized upon. Blocking with the
elbows in a fixed position has been proven successful.
The fixed position differs from the high-elbow technique
in that it is assumed from a crouched position on the foul
lane. The hands are placed on the thighs and the elbows
are extended outward. It is advantageous because the
elbows are placed in front of the opponent before the
play starts.

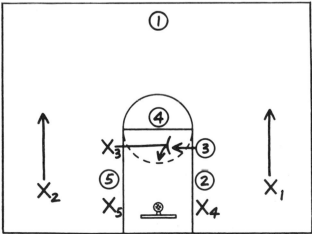

Diagram 43

6

FAST BREAK FROM
THE MATCH-UP

One of the quickest and cleverest ways to score in basketball is the fast break. Even a team playing the percentage game will have occasion to employ this explosive offensive weapon whether it comes about by chance or by a planned pattern.

Opportunities for fast breaking are less evident today for several reasons. Rebounding is much more competitive at all levels of the game. The rebound starts the fast break so a team that does not get the ball off the board can forget it. The shooter is not forcing his shot as he did a decade ago and consequently is making a much higher percentage. Good shooting cuts down rebound situations and reduces the fast break opportunity. Modern defense has also cut the number of fast break opportunities from the foul shot and the jump ball, and is doing a better job stopping the outlet pass which is so important in the breaking game.

The loose ball or stolen pass present fast break situations that are very effective simply because it is difficult to organize group defense against free-lance play of this type.

Defensive reaction to the intercepted pass, the jump ball and the loose ball is difficult to teach, especially to the young boy. So, the fast break has its place in the game and a coach had better be prepared to defend against it regardless of his intentions to use it as an offensive weapon. I always employ some type of fast break with my offensive attack, often ignoring the available material or team speed. Cleverness is needed, however, when team speed is not apparent.

Many coaches contend that they use nothing but the control game. Nevertheless their teams get baskets from fast break situations no matter how close they plan the strict control theory. I have heard many coaches say there is no place for the careless play and I agree with them. The statement is more true with the fast break than with other phases of the game even though it may not seem that way on the surface. The fast break requires a high degree of organization because the fundamentals of ball handling, passing, shooting, and footwork are important.

At one time, the lone objective of the fast break was to score before the defense could get set, but today the use of trailers and a planned scheme of activity present opportunities to score from the break without speed.

From the basic Match-Up formation the outlet pass area is easy to find, the lanes become accessible, and the trailer or trailers are available according to the desires of the coach and his team's abilities. The Match-Up is known for its unusual defensive theory but it lends great effect to the breaking game.

THE SPECIALIST THEORY

It would be wonderful to have five men on the same team who could rebound, handle the ball as it moves down court, and always be in the left lane if left-handed or in the right lane if right-handed, but this occurs only by chance unless they happen to be playing a relative position on defense when the break is started. Many fast break attempts have been stalled when the big cumbersome player has attempted to handle the middle position coming down court. Therefore, I believe that every player should be a specialist from his position on the fast break. No matter how thorough fundamental drills may be, every player cannot learn to play every position with adeptness. When the duties of the various fast break positions are outlined so that each player may get the most from his limitations, saved practice time can be guided toward other areas. At the same time the fast break becomes much easier to teach and more effective.

It is less difficult and less time consuming to teach one or two players to handle the middle position on the fast break than it is to teach the complete squad. At the same time the middle-man is learning his position, the big boys can be working on getting off the back line of the defensive formation to make the three-lane or trailer situation complete. Naturally this places the best rebounders under the basket when the opponent shoots.

Maximum results from the available material is the goal of every coach. The Match-Up presents a challenge that will show immediate success when the material is evaluated properly. Every year there will be several boys that can play two or three different positions. One of the great thrills of coaching is to witness success in the form of wins when a boy gets the maximum from his physical and mental abilities by adjusting to various positions.

LOCATION OF THE PLAYERS

See Diagram 44, page 167, for the defensive location of each player before they come out on the fast break.

Best ball-handler

The fast-break-man or best ball handler should be at the left-front position in order to expedite the movement of the ball at the start of the break. As mentioned in Chapter 3 he will have to be a good defensive player because he will be carrying more than his share of the defensive load in addition to the area he will have to cover to receive the ball. Regardless, he will be near the area in which he starts the break if it is tapped out or even if passed to other locations. He will also get fast break opportunities from the long rebound. If the outlet pass is made to either side he will be in the middle to take a release pass after the break is started.

Right front man

This player should be right-handed since he will be moving to the right lane and will do a great deal of the shooting off the break. The front location naturally gives him a start that is needed to get in the outlet pass location and then down court. If the outlet pass is made to his position he must be careful when passing to the middle lane. After the ball is moved to the side by the rebounding team, the middle of the court is usually jammed. At the start of the break most coaches instruct their boys to get back on defense by coming down the middle of the court so that interceptions can be made and the ball can be cut off or slowed down. Over the years my teams have picked up important baskets, when the opponent concentrated on the fast-break-man, by having the right-front player dribble down the right side. If he is stopped he may pass to the trailer, or eventually get the ball to the fast-break-man once the defense concentrates on the ball. An effective, moving short jump shot is a necessity for the side lanes when they are cut-off at the basket.

Left corner man

Most likely, this player will be the best all-around player on the squad. His defensive requirements were mentioned in Chapter 3. Speed and agility are very important because he must rebound and eventually become part of the front line on the break. It takes guts, hustle, and pride to get the job done from this position. It is not necessary that he be left-handed but the natural side of the court is always best. If the right front player is left-handed these two players can exchange lanes of the fast break. Many times the player in this position will not be in on the fast break because the two front players will have the ball down court if he is the rebounder. If this situation arises one of the trailers can fill his lane and he may become a trailer.

At Pompano Beach High School tradition alone supplied us with a boy who wanted to hold down this particular job. It started during my first year as head coach there with a boy who couldn't shoot very well, couldn't pass very well, couldn't dribble very well, but could make a driving lay-up with accuracy that was far from the desired shooting form. He happened to have enough hustle for several boys. Early in the season, Larry Coker, who later played football for Wake Forest, said he could rebound, get the ball out, get down court, and run laps around the free throw circle while waiting for the rest of the team to get down on the fast break. The papers picked up this comment and started a tradition that supplied us with boys that thought they were this fast. In addition it was an excellent morale builder and kept us fast-break-minded.

The abilities of the remaining two positions will determine the type of trailers to be used. Trailers are always necessary when the front line of the break is stymied once the ball has reached the offensive end of the court. On several occasions I have been blessed with over-all team speed and employed a trailer on each side of the ball. At other times I have had some big boys who were lucky to get down the floor at all. They would come through often with a follow-up rebound basket and sometimes score from a delay situation while the opponent scrambled to set up their defense thinking the fast break had been stopped.

Middle position

The best rebounder and most rugged of the big boys should be in the middle position. Most rebounds will come off in his area and it is important that he stay near the basket He should be a trailer and sometimes fill in the left lane.

Right corner man

The slowest player on the team will probably be in the right corner. Naturally he should have some size, and be tough on the boards. He is in an ideal position to be the safety man. He may still be a trailer but will be the needed security if the other team recovers a fumble or steals a pass. A tall man is not a necessity for this position but he must have abilities to gain the ball and get it out quickly so the fast break pattern can be started.

All of these positions can be handled without blinding speed. Sometimes too much speed can be damaging. Of course it is always good to have two or three fast players regardless of how effective the trailer may be.

LANES

The Match-Up emphasizes the three-lane straight line controlled break. The players come out of their defensive positions and go straight toward the basket, very seldom crossing paths.

The emphasis is simplicity and, viewing the court lengthwise, the lanes are divided into right, middle, and left. The object is to fill the lanes as quickly as possible with little variation of personnel. I am very much interested in who fills the lane since emphasis is put on the specialist's theory.

The fast-break-man comes down the middle lane and will handle the ball about eighty per cent of the time. Speed and good ball handling are the keynotes of this lane. I like the fast-break-man to dribble the ball a great deal because this seems to set up the outside lanes better and makes the trailer more effective. If the middle man is not a good dribbler, it is best to move the ball to the side and then back to the middle a few times to take the pressure off the middle man. Once the ball gets to the scoring area it should be in the hands of the fast-break-man somewhere near the middle lane area. I prefer him to stop at the foul line for several reasons. If he is an effective shooter from this stopping area, it will open up the side lanes. If the ball gets tied up under the basket they usually can pass out to him for a high percentage shot. He may be used as a screen by the trailers and will be in excellent position to pass off to them as they move through. Occasionally it will be necessary for him to go all the way to the basket but with today's defense he will very seldom get the wide open lay-up.

When the ball reaches the foul line area the defense will be there most of the time. The ball handler should charge the defense with a strong burst of speed and as he meets resistance, challenge them by moving the ball slightly to one side of the circle. When the defense declares by pulling to one side with the ball the side lanes may open up or enough room will be made available for the trailer to get through.

The location of the side lanes are the same as they would be from most fast break patterns. The side players come straight down the court to the foul circle area. Once in this area they cut at a straight angle for the basket. A good target to familiarize the beginners with is the area between the backboard and the back part of the rim. The six inches from the board to the rim is the desired line of action when attempting the shot but the cut must be made from the side at the foul line extended.

When the ball is in the side lanes the change of pace a dribble with short and full strides can be emphasized.

TRAILER

We will assume at this point that the first three players down court have effectively moved the ball into the area of the basket but have failed to make a scoring attempt. Success is now in the hands of the trailer.

I have found it very difficult to teach key verbal signals to set up the trailer. Dummy drills should be the first step used in developing timing but a shout or yell from the trailer, at the right time, helps when he is delayed.

I prefer the single trailer because he has more room to set up his options. The other player back can do a full time job of playing the safety.

If the center defensive position is used as the trailer he should follow about ten or fifteen feet behind the fast-break-man. He may score from several options. If he is slow getting down court he may use the middle man as a screen and shoot over him if the ball has been passed back just before he reaches the foul circle area. He may catch the defense standing by taking a hand-off from the middle-man and burst through for the lay-up. This particular situation happens sometimes because the defense momentarily interprets the pause of the ball as a successful attempt at stopping the break. If the ball is in the hands of one of the side lanes the trailer may receive a pass from them as he goes through. In addition he has an opportunity to screen for the side lanes. If they have room to drive for the basket he is always available for the rebound or a second effort for the basket.

There seems to be a decrease in the use of two trailers where the three-lane fast break is involved. Two trailers take more time and work to develop and these positions require excellent alertness as far as protection against interceptions and loose balls is concerned. Most scoring opportunities from double trailers come from passes made by the side lanes. When two trailers crash the board, the middle lane should be responsible for the safety position which could leave a team wide open against a long pass after the opponent retrieves the ball.

Diagram 44

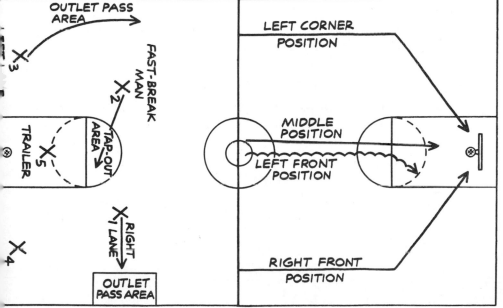

The trailer play is a pretty one to watch but it takes split-second timing. Without it your fast break will only be two thirds as effective as it should be.

TAP-OUT OR PASS-OUT

Up to this point we have talked about how individual assignments make the fast break effective. We are now at a point: no ball—no break. The fast break, probably more than any other phase of the game, is developed by progressive steps. Rebounding was discussed in Chapter 2 but this brings us to a situation that has drawn criticism, brought success, and a few failures. It is the first and a very important phase of the breaking game. Should the ball be passed out to start the break, should it be tapped out to a designated area, or should a combination of these out-let passes be employed? Some coaches say they would not take the chance of tapping the ball out. If you have speed and ball handling and no height advantage it seems as though a lot of good material will be going to waste if some method of getting the ball out is not developed. In other words, tap out if you can't throw out. Even if you can dominate the boards there are many occasions when the ball can be tapped out to a desired area even though you cannot get both hands on the ball.

One handed jump is higher

It has been proven by experiment that a player can get up in the air from six to ten inches higher with one hand than he can with both hands. This point would seem to favor tapping out for the smaller teams. When the ball is passed out the opposition has time to react and get down court. If it is tapped out successfully you will have the jump on your opponent and the needed two or three steps which make the start of the break much more successful. Even with constant work on tapping-out, many situations will occur that require the first move to be a pass to either side or to the middle. It is very easy to coordinate the two outlet attacks. Many times I tell my boys to pass out when they can take it off the board and to tap-out when they cannot control the ball. See the Tap-Out, Pass-Out Drill, Diagram 59, page 192.

Marshall University made the tap-out famous when they won the N.A.I.B. Tournament at Kansas City in 1947. They virtually blew their opponent off the court with a quick tap-out and good ball handling. Their speed wasn't devastating but the tap-out gave them a few strides and good ball handling did the rest.

Tap to the top of the free throw circle is easiest

Tapping to the top of the free-throw circle is the most feasible location because it sets the fast-break-man up so well. From this position he may make a release pass to either side or move the ball down court with a dribble as his teammates fill their lanes. Over the years I have had the ball tapped to the side and/or to other locations. However, this type of tapping must be practiced, practiced, practiced. I have found that it takes a team with good mental reactions to change the tapping location during the process of a game. I have experienced three teams in fifteen years that perfected this type of tapping.

The most important thing in tapping the ball is training the fast-break-man, who is the usual receiver, to get into position for the tap. Many teams will assign one player to steal the tap but there are several preparations that will help overcome such a predicament. In the first place, my team prepares for the tap-out and fast break during the complete season, which usually involves about twenty-five or thirty games, while the opponent has only two occasions a year to stop it. Needless to say the play should be perfected enough to hold an advantage.

Defending against the pick of play

Many coaches have asked, "What do you do when your opponent stations a strong boy in the area of the tap-out?" This type pick-off play is used quite often by the opposition but once again progressive steps are practiced by the fast-break-men to make the tap-out successful.

When the opponent stations himself low (near the foul line) to intercept the tap-out, the fast-break-man moves to a position perpendicular to, but on the same line as the opponent. When this position is established, the fast-break-man has a clear view to the direction of the tap-out. If the ball is tapped short, the fast-break-man rolls to the inside of the opponent. If the ball is tapped high, the fast-break-man rolls to the outside of the opponent and gets the tap-out at or beyond the head of the circle. The fast-break-man must spread his feet fairly wide, awaiting the tap, and should, if possible, attempt to move his opponent out of position. (See Diagram 45.)

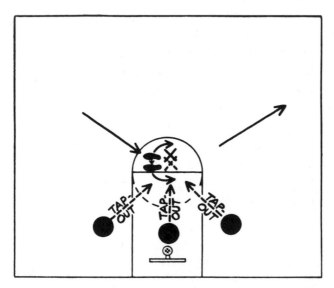

Diagram 45

Diagram 46

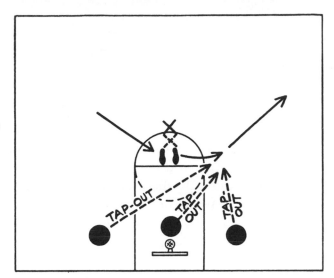

The positioning procedure above can be used with the following tapping situations.

The off center tap-out is a variation which can be implemented when the opponent is playing for the center tap and is doing a successful job of stopping the fast break. The location of the tap-out may need to be changed for only a short period of time. If it is more effective at the new location, stay with it. The side to which the ball should be tapped is pre-determined. If the opponent sets high the fast-break-man rolls to one side, forcing the opponent, if possible, to the opposite side. (See Diagram 46.)

If the opposition sends two men to intercept the tap-out, the off-center tap is a possible answer. The fast-break-man stations himself in front of one of the opponents, which is pre-determined, and rolls to the outside. The ball is tapped to the pre-determined area. (See Diagram 47.)

The reader will note that very little emphasis has been placed upon initiating the fast break after a rebound with the pass. I am aware this is a vital technique in the breaking game. The Match-Up defense works so well with a tap-out that I favor this move as the primary method of getting the ball out for the start of the break.

Coaches who are suspicious of the merits of the tap-out

will find that the pass-out from the Match-Up is more effective than from most other defensive alignments. In order to concentrate upon methods that have been effective for me, I will not dwell on the fundamentals of the pass-out theory. Much material has been written on this subject. Naturally there are occasions when the pass-out is a must. A team can develop mastery of this skill through the Tap-out Pass-out Drill discussed in this chapter.

Lead pass drills are needed to develop the pass-out to the left lane area since the receiver will be on the move from the back line of defense. Some type of long, quick pass drill should be employed to develop the pass to the right side since he will be located in a more or less congested area and does not move down court until the ball is successfully tapped out or taken off the board and passed out.

Now the reader should have an idea of how the Match-Up starts the fast break from the rebound. Now let's take a look at fast break activity from other opportunities that do not start from the rebound.

Diagram 47

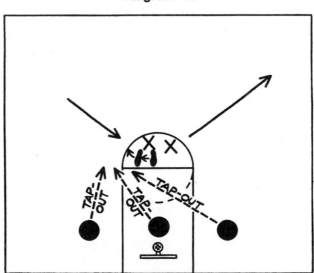

FAST BREAK—CENTER JUMP

When a team attempts the fast break from the center jump, in most instances, they must be able to control the tap. There are many jump-ball situations with many different possibilities which make it relatively easy for a coach to adjust his material according to ball handling and other team abilities. Consequently we will discuss a few of the more successful fast break plays that I have observed or used effectively. These methods may also be employed at the free throw circles.

The logical place to tap on the circle is the place where two of your players are together with no opposing player between them. Many teams play for possession when they have a tapping advantage but with fast breaking material I like to maintain the ball and also score before the opponent sets up their basic defense.

Very seldom have I gone along with the theory of keeping every player on the circle when control of the tap is assured. When controlling the tap a team should be able to make the opponent play their game by tapping away from the circle in various directions, forcing the defense to cover more area.

The fast break play can also be developed when control is not evident. If the scouting report indicates that the opponent likes to tap to a special area or player then the jumper should be able to tap in the same direction as the opponent. A fast break situation can develop because any contact with the ball will carry it to a location away from the circle due to the force by both jumpers. Many times I prefer to go with the tap with my weaker jumpers or at any time I am over-matched.

Forming a pocket

Several years ago I employed a fast break from the center jump that involved forming a pocket in the area where the ball was to be tapped. The forming of this pocket required that we have two of our boys together with no opponent between them. We always stationed the two boys who were forming the pocket on the front half of the circle with the fast-break-man's right foot against his teammate's left foot. If our opponent demanded that we open up and let them between these two players we would gladly do so and then move one of the back players up to form a new pocket with the fast-break-man on the front side of the circle. It was a simple game

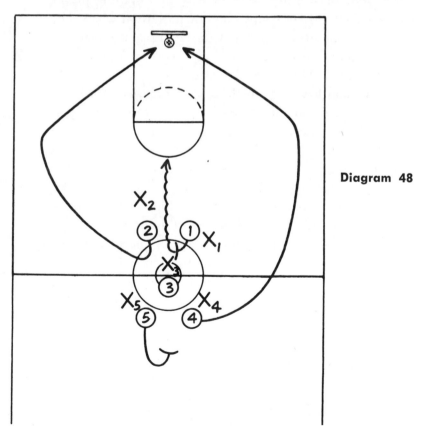

Diagram 48

of cat-and-mouse but we seemed to always get our pocket which would lead to possession and the fast break. (See Diagram 48.)

METHOD

1. (1) is the fast-break-man and the tap receiver. He forms his half of the pocket by stepping in front of X1 with his left foot, pivoting off his right foot. He must make sure that he has a strong position so that X1 will not force him off balance or out of position. When he receives the ball he may pass to (4), (2), or dribble down the middle to the foul line.

2. (2) forms the other half of the pocket by stepping into the circle with a forward pivot off his right foot. He screens his man and moves out to fill the left lane. He must move out to the left lane position in order to have the proper floor balance for the break.

3. (4) moves wide down the right lane when his team has possession. He is in the position to receive a scoring pass from (1).

4. (3) makes a strong downward tap and then trails down the middle of the court.

5. (5) stays near the circle, alert to pick up a deflected tap and serves as the safety man.

The long tap

In 1962, at Pompano Beach Senior High School, we had two boys on the squad who were six feet seven inches tall, assuring us of the center tap. We toyed with several fast break situations from the center jump and through trial and error came up with a formation that placed two of our players at the top of our free throw circle. As the

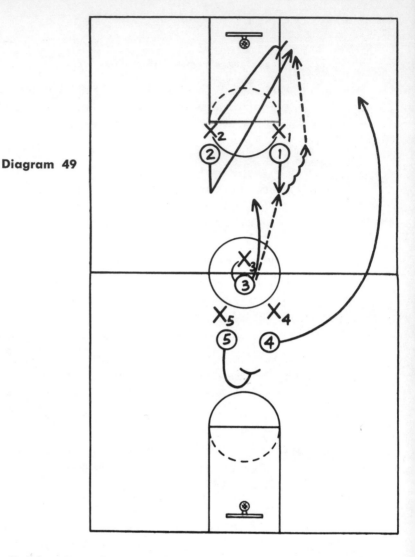

Diagram 49

official prepared to toss the ball these two players would move forward two steps. If the opponent played in front of them we would use the long tap over their heads for the easy lay-up. If the opponent played behind us we used a fast break play that scored many times. Early in the year we set a goal to score before three seconds had ticked off the clock. We scored seven times that year before three seconds had been registered on the clock and many more times within four seconds.

When using the play in Diagram 49, you must be assured of a strong tapping advantage since the ball must be tapped twice the distance of the usual tap.

METHOD

1. (1) moves up two steps and receives the tap. He is careful to screen out X1 who is behind him. He makes a reverse pivot facing the basket with the ball. He may drive with a one-on-one situation, pass to (2) under the basket, or pass to (4) coming down the right lane.
2. (2) moves under the basket facing the ball and staying in front of his defensive player, X2. If he does not receive a pass for the shot he moves to the opposite side of the board for rebound position which will come from the fast break shot.
3. (3) taps to (1) when the defense locates in these positions and moves to the basket for a possible rebound or trailer play.
4. (4) moves out to the side to fill the right lane and a possible release pass from (1).
5. (5) is the safety man.

The tap can be made to either side in order to keep the opponent guessing. In Diagram 50 it is made to the right side.

METHOD

1. (1) moves up as before and then moves over to screen for (4) after (4) receives the ball. He then rolls off toward the basket for a possible lead pass or rebound.
2. (2) moves under the basket as before. If he does not receive a quick pass he moves to the opposite side of the ball getting good rebound position.

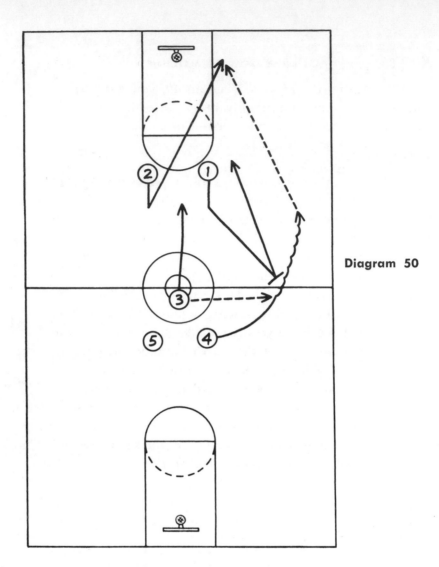

Diagram 50

3. (3) taps the ball outside and moves down the middle of the court as before.

4. (4) moves to the side carefully timing the ball. He may pass to (2) under the basket, drive after a screen from (1), or pass to (1) after the roll off. He may also pass to (3) moving down the middle.

5. (5) is the safety man. If this play is run to the left, (5) will make the same move as (4).

THE QUICK SECOND TAP

Occasionally during the course of a game you may spot a team playing tight on the circle even though you will be controlling the tap. When this happens a second tap down court will set up an easy basket. This play is as old as basketball but every season I have managed to get two or three baskets with some quick thinking involved. It takes no practice and can be diagrammed on the side line at a time out or just before the start of a period. Better yet, it is a good idea to give the play some name that can be called when the defense is spotted playing very tight.

Diagram 51

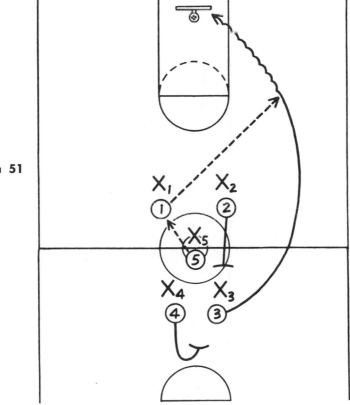

The player making the second tap must be instructed to make a strong, aggressive play rather than a soft, lofty tap that can be anticipated or intercepted. (See Diagram 51.)

METHOD

1. (5) taps to (1).
2. (1) taps firmly down court to (3) who has cut off the screen set by (2).
3. (4) is the safety man.

Diagram 52

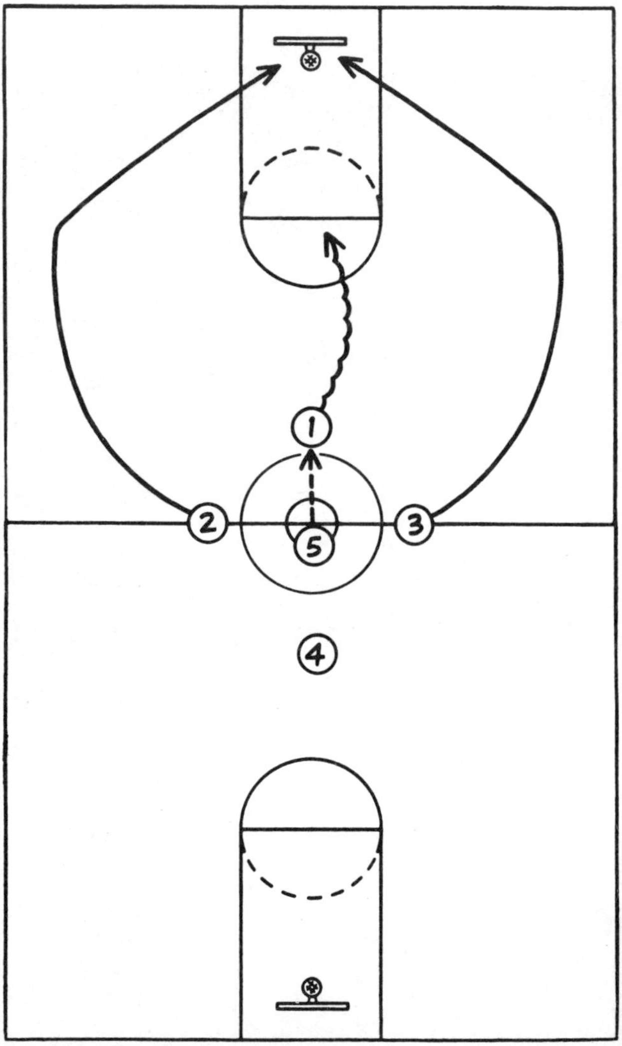

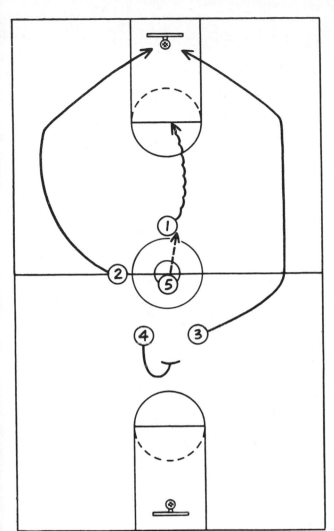

WIDELY USED FAST BREAK JUMP FORMATIONS

The three most common formations for fast breaking from the jump ball are the 2-1-2 formation, the 1-3-1 formation, and the 2-2-1 formation. The 1-3-1 and 2-2-1 formations present situations that will have two players on the same team together without anyone between them. The 2-1-2 set-up has this spot located in back of the jumper but a tap to the front side will be effective if the receiver screens his man out as he goes after the ball.

The jumper should be responsible for checking locations and finding the spot where two of his teammates are together. It is a good idea to have the jumper step back from the jumping area momentarily so his teammates will have time to establish a tapping area. (See Diagrams 52 and 53.)

FREE THROW FAST BREAK

The fast break after a made or missed foul shot has caused some anxiety on my part as a coach. At one time my teams employed the break from each of these situations, without much concern with charting its success or failure. Later, when our charts did indicate that we were not scoring as well as we were from the rebound and other fast break plays we decided that something must be done to counteract the usual defense that opposes this type of fast break. The opposition is in a position to slow the ball down since most teams have one or two players back on defense and the remainder of the squad at the foul lane which presents excellent positioning to stop the break. If the opponent has done any scouting the outlet pass can be slowed down, if not intercepted. In addition they will have defense waiting at the other end of the court or at half court.

The familiar pattern of placing players at each side of the foul lane or placing everyone on the foul lane to start the fast break is still good because the fast break lanes are easy to locate. In this instance you must be a great deal faster than your opponent or have them out-classed with ball handling because they are located well enough to stop the break at any or all of the following areas: the outlet area, the middle court area, or the scoring area.

The tap-out on the missed foul shot could be the equal-

izer. In addition, placing two men on the offensive end of
the court for pattern situations will cause the opponent
some anxiety, since they must adjust to something different. The success of a fast break with this situation will
rest primarily on the shoulders of the fast-break-man. He
will not have the help of a release pass, and must dribble
the ball the full length of the court. The dribble invites
the opposition to cut the ball off at mid-court with a
double team play. However, this move usually causes
them to be out-numbered in the scoring area when the
ball is passed over the intended trap.

From the made free throw

Let's take first things first—the outlet pass on a made
foul shot. Since most players are right-handed, it is best
to designate the player near the basket to throw the ball
in bounds, but it should be to his natural side. Let's sup-
pose the throw-in player is right-handed. He must take
the ball out of the net, being careful to get it out of bounds
as quickly as possible. If the ball comes through the net
awkwardly, have the opposite player tap it out to the
throw-in player. These situations must be practiced in
order to save valuable time. The pass to the fast-break-
man is made almost to midcourt on the right side since
the player throwing in is right-handed. The long pass is
important because it covers a great deal of floor space and
saves time. A long accurate passer is needed at this position. The throw-in player will then become the safety
man during the fast break.

The other player next to the basket on the lane is des-
signated as the eventual screener when the ball reaches
the scoring area. He checks to see that the ball is in the
hands of the throw-in player and then moves down court
to the right side of his own free throw line. Later the fast-

break-man may use him as a screen or he may roll to the basket for a pass. Regardless of his use as a screen or roll-off-player he will be in excellent rebound position.

The player who handles the ball down court gets into position on the foul lane to cover the foul shooter in case the shot is missed or a long rebound occurs. After covering the shooter he moves across court and up the side looking for the lead pass. Some teams try to break up the play by covering this pass, so he must be alert to change his location if needed. As mentioned before he must dribble the ball down court. He may move close behind the screener who is headed for the foul line which could help protect the ball.

Two players are placed at the opposite end of the court which will usually draw two opposing players with them. The moves from these positions take a great deal of timing. They line up in the corners opposite each other. The distance from the corner base-line will depend upon individual speed. (See Diagram 54.)

The player in the left corner, (1), moves up the side-line to the top of the foul circle extended when the foul shot is made. He then takes a sharp turn off his left foot moving across the top of the circle, just touching the line,

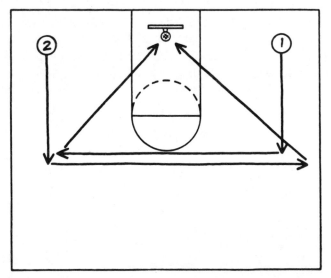

Diagram 54

as he goes to the opposite side of the court. Upon reaching the opposite side of the court he makes an oblique turn off his left foot going directly toward the basket.

At the same time, the player in the right corner, (2), moves up the right side making his cuts off the right foot, and then across court one yard outside the circle, careful not to contact his teammate.

A good rule of thumb to determine the movement of these two players is that the screener and fast-break-man should move into the circle area just after the two corner players pass or open up.

Diagram 55

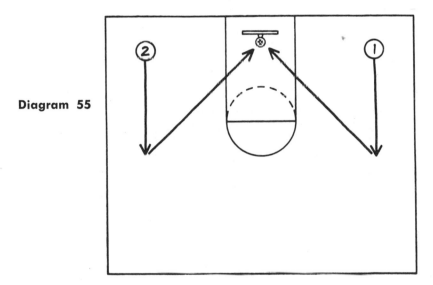

An excellent change from the movement just mentioned is to have these positions move up the side as they did before, but instead of crossing, cut for the basket from the same side of the court. (See Diagram 55.)

From the missed free throw

If the foul shot is missed, the fast-break-man will prob-

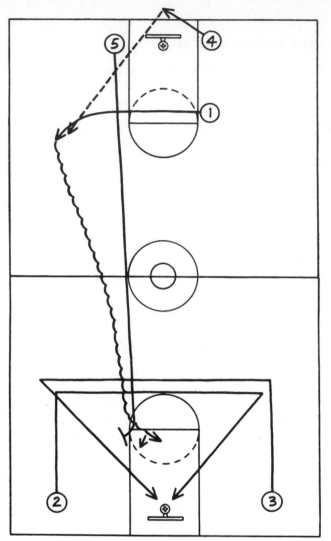

Diagram 56

ably not have the screener. It is difficult for him to get down court since the ball is tapped out on the missed shot.

On the tap-out, the fast-break-man moves across court to cover the foul shooter and then to the side. If the ball is tapped to the side accurately, his movement across the lane will give him some momentum which will help get the ball down court quicker. If the opposition is covering the play the tapping area can be changed by some sort of signal. Usually a number will be sufficient to designate the tapping area.

Sometimes it is difficult for a young squad to get the most out of this particular play due to the time it takes to properly synchronize the movement. It may be well worth the time involved to use it during tournament play or for a special game. In one game at Newberry College we scored nine times from this play proving that it is difficult to stop unless your opponent is prepared to defend against it.

When developing the fast break play from the foul shot, it should be broken down with emphasis on each area—the outlet pass, getting the ball down court with the cutters available, and the scoring situation. The use of a stop watch will take the guesswork out of player location. (See Diagram 56 for the complete play.)

SOME FAST BREAK DRILLS

There are many drills that make the fast break effective and most can be incorporated with basic fundamentals. Any drill that involves the lead-pass, the pass-and-cut play, the aggressive lay-up, and the rebound outlet-pass play will improve the fast break game. The drills that follow are important because they unite the Match Up and the fast break with the outlet, the down court movement, and the scoring attempt.

Tap-out lay-up drill

The Tap-Out Lay-up Drill incorporates the tap-out, the fast break pass from the foul line, and the driving lay-up. After the fundamentals of the lay-up have been thoroughly explained and each boy examined and corrected, the drill is in order. It should be used daily and is an excellent pre-game warm-up drill.

Diagram 57

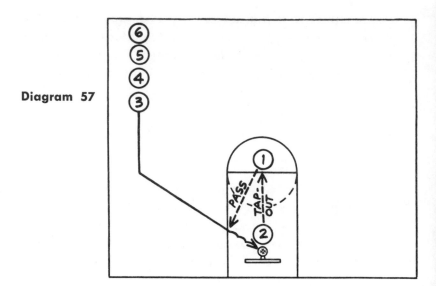

METHOD

1. (3) drives down the right lane to the foul line extended and cuts for the basket receiving a pass from (1), who is on the foul line, for the lay-up. After he shoots he replaces (2) under the basket.

2. (2) waits under the basket for the shot and taps the made or missed shot to (1) at the foul line. He then replaces (1) and becomes the next passer. The tap-out of a made basket is not a normal situation but it does accustom the team to react to the tap-out and permits practice to the various tapping areas.

3. (1) takes the tap-out and passes to the lay-up player. He then moves to the opposite side of the court to form a new line.

Follow the lay-up drill

Most young boys lack the aggressiveness that is needed at the tail end of the fast break. The best example of the type of aggressiveness that is needed was demonstrated by West Virginia University when Rod Hundley was handling the fast break during the early fifties. I studied several films of their games in which the defense, on many occasions, was down court waiting for "Hot Rod" and his teammates to come in for the lay-up or short shot off the break. West Virginia seemed to come down court at three-fourths speed trying to get their lane alignment, which included a trailer down the middle. Then, with a sudden change of pace, they burst from the top of the circle in the front court and through to the basket with a speed which seemed to catch the opposition standing. Many times the defense would get a hand on the ball but Mountaineer aggressiveness would come through with constant baskets. Defensive harassment did not seem to bother them as their momentum and ability to shoot the strong lay-up paid a high dividend.

Later when I tried to develop this type of aggressiveness with group drills, the point that West Virginia University had put over so well came about slowly. Three line drills and team drills that had the defense stationed at the end of the court helped my boys get the alignment and timing but not the consistent basket. After some time I suddenly realized that aggressive play is primarily an individual ability. My boys needed some personal pride that I could not develop with team drills. Consequently, Follow-The-Lay-Up Drill was the answer. Improvement from this drill at the high school level was rewarding but during my tenure at Newberry College it made our fast break respectable, though we had very little speed.

The drill involves some unintentional contact but will make the game situation less difficult because play of this nature would be regarded as a foul during an actual game.

It is advisable to have the players choose a partner of equal speed and ability but on occasion a fun drill will build morale by pairing off the smaller players with the larger players. Either of these line-ups will help develop the lay-up under the most difficult duress and harassment.

Diagram 58

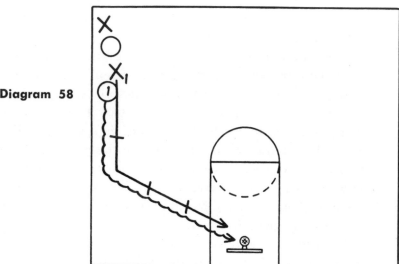

METHOD

1. (1) dribbles down the right lane to the foul circle extended and cuts for the basket. He may shoot on either side of the basket using the board.

2. X1 lines up two steps behind (1). He follows him closely, trying to break up the lay-up or drive movement. He cannot take a short cut and must make his interference from the side or from behind the player with the ball. His main purpose is to make the lay-up more difficult by using a strong block with little regard to contact.

3. A new line is formed on the opposite side of the court after all players have taken their turn. When (1) has attempted a lay-up from both sides he exchanges places with X1.

Three line drills

The half court three line attack must be practiced from the start of the season in order to make the front court attack reach its maximum effectiveness. A full court drill can be coordinated with the half court drill in order to adjust floor balance. Habits and traits of each player are different. A player will make some moves at close quarters that are not needed when moving down court at various speeds. Three line drills present opportunities for each player to familiarize himself with the habits of his teammates.

Three-on-two and four-on-three drills must be practiced daily when a large part of the offense is the fast break. A four-on-three drill will involve a trailer in which timing is more difficult.

It is a good idea, when playing away from home, to get on court a few minutes before the home team. During this time a team has an opportunity to run a dummy full court three line drill a few times. This period will give the team the feel of the whole court and its surroundings. If this cannot be done, the three line half-court drill is a must during the pre-game warm-up for a fast breaking team. Since the three line drills are so common and have been printed so many times we will omit diagraming them. A detailed treatment of these drills would not be a waste of time even though the fast break may not be in the scheme of the overall offensive attack. They are good conditioning drills and excellent practice for various fundamentals.

The tap-out pass-out drill

The tap-out should never be the sole outlet for the fast break. Near the end of a close game it is best to instruct the team to take no chances. Naturally possession is important, so instruction to tap-out only if the ball cannot be taken off the board is in order. When playing against a team which has superior size or when behind by a large margin the tap-out is in order. The difference in size and score can be made up quickly with some quick baskets from the fast break. The change over from the tap-out to the pass-out takes practice and, like other parts of the breaking game, will seem ragged at first.

The Tap-Out Pass-Out Drills are most effective when used the day before a game but they should not be employed against opposition at this time. Early in the season resistance is needed, but timing is more important the day before a game and the possibility of injury should be kept to a minimum. This drill conditions a team's reactions to make the change over from the tap-out to the pass-out under the pressures of a game situation.

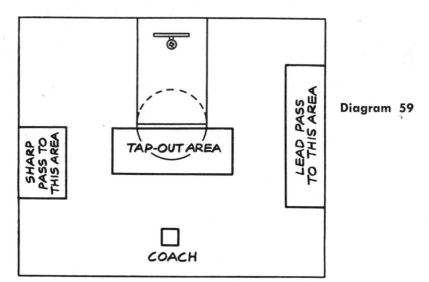

Diagram 59

METHOD

1. A cover is placed over the basket to assure rebound opportunities.
2. The players locate in their Match-Up positions.
3. The manager, or coach, shoots the ball and while it is in the air he yells out the type of outlet pass to be made. If he signals tap-out, the ball is tapped to the proper area and a dummy fast break is run full court. If he signals outlet pass, the ball is passed sharply to the right side of the court where the dummy fast break starts. This move usually necessitates a second pass to the fast-break-man. If the manager signals lead-pass, the outlet is made to the left side of the court as the left back player takes it on the move down the left side.

7

SCOUTING
AND CHARTING

A MUST FOR THE MATCH-UP

In order to enjoy the full measure of success from the Match-Up, it is necessary to devise adequate systems of scouting and charting. This chapter, divided into two parts, will be devoted to explaining the methods which have enabled me to effectively exploit the Match-Up. Neither system is overly elaborate nor complicated. Both are simple but highly functional.

SCOUTING

The extent to which a basketball scouting program can be carried is virtually without limitation. One needs only to look at the great emphasis today on scouting in the colleges. "A coach can no longer send his boys into a contest partially or totally blind to the potentialities of the opponents." Statements like this are representative of the feelings of most college coaches.

Intensive film analysis is no longer the province of

football alone. I have found that for special situations (pre-tournament preparation, arch rivalries, etc.) there is no substitute for a careful film study of the opposition. When money is available this emphasis should be placed on every game. Other automated devices, aside from the movie camera, are being employed in scouting today. One of the most recent to gain popularity is the compact transistor operated tape recorder which allows a scout to relay, verbally, a vast quantity of information without having to take his eyes from the stream of activity on the court.

With all the modern additions to basketball scouting, I have found the most reliable and most practical system to be one that affords us clear, visual analysis. Our basic scouting materials are an ordinary manila folder, some shot charts, two clip boards, and plenty of extra pencils. The following will show how these very minimum essentials are implemented to form a complete picture of our opposition's strengths and weaknesses.

Two scouts are necessary to make adequate use of the materials. One, either the head or assistant coach, should assume the most responsible role—that of recording team and individual movements. The second observer can handle the less demanding duty of keeping shot charts and can also lend verbal assistance to the other scout. Both should arrive early enough to observe the preliminary game when it is played. Often one can get a very valuable briefing on varsity movements by paying attention to these contests. An early arrival also gives the serious scout a chance to make notes on individual shooting habits during the pre-game warm-up. We try to select a seating area where we have a good view of the entire floor—preferably high up and toward the center of the court.

The manila folder, prepared in advance as shown in Diagram 60 (parts 1 and 2), is the foundation of our

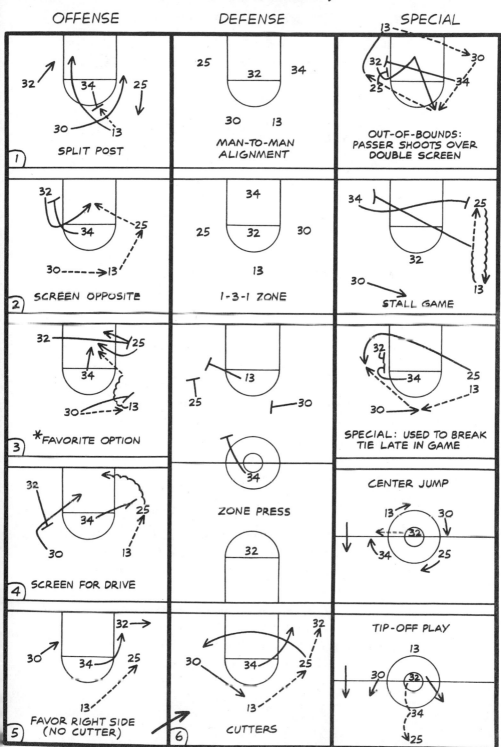

OFFENSE | DEFENSE | SPECIAL

1. SPLIT POST | MAN-TO-MAN ALIGNMENT | OUT-OF-BOUNDS: PASSER SHOOTS OVER DOUBLE SCREEN

2. SCREEN OPPOSITE | 1-3-1 ZONE | STALL GAME

3. *FAVORITE OPTION | | SPECIAL: USED TO BREAK TIE LATE IN GAME

4. SCREEN FOR DRIVE | ZONE PRESS | CENTER JUMP

5. FAVOR RIGHT SIDE (NO CUTTER) | 6. CUTTERS | TIP-OFF PLAY

scouting report. It is divided into three general areas. A description and explanation of each area follows:

Area I—team patterns

This area, which covers the entire left side of the folder, is subdivided into three categories—team offenses, team defenses, and special team situations. The first category, team offenses, gives the information which is so vital to the Match-Up theory. A team that relies on pattern-style play can become easy prey to the Match-Up if the scout can competently record the basic offensive movements and options in this area. Naturally, this category is of less importance against a freelance opponent; if this is the case, another area of the scouting report assumes major importance—Individual Information—which will be discussed later.

In noting patterned offensive movement, it is essential to indicate the defense which is being employed by the other team. As soon as the defense is determined, it is best to take an over-all view of the opponent—trying to conclude if a basic continuity is obvious. The formation can then be diagramed and, as the movement and options begin to unfold, they can be added with little difficulty. Be sure to "star" favorite options or situations where the ball is forced into a particular player.

If a definite continuity is not immediately visible, but there is evidence of pattern style play, it is best to sketch the formation and then the complete movement of each player, individually, until the over-all style begins to take shape. A team that employs a style of play which capitalizes on two or three-man patterns often gives the illusion of a five-man continuity to anyone but the keen observer.

While the Match-Up seems to encourage zone tactics, many times a baffled opponent will resort to man-to-man strategy. Thus, it is important to observe adequately both the zone and man-to-man patterns of a potential opponent even if this necessitates more than one scouting visit. As the Match-Up thrives on scouting information, more knowledge of the opponent makes for better defensive preparation.

The second category under Team Patterns is team defense. If the opponent uses a man-to-man defense, this section of the chart does not lose its importance. The area in which a player picks up the opponent is important. This can be designated by placing the defensive players' numbers on the chart as you would when recording a zone defense. The point to be made here is, how can you take advantage of the size of the opponent by moving the smaller players under the basket and the larger players away from the basket. (See this category in Diagram 60, Part 1, page 197.)

For the team that uses a zone or zone variation, this category is probably more effective in determining offensive strategy.

Special defenses, traps, and full court zone presses, can be carefully diagramed in this area. Of particular note is the area in which the defense encourages the ball to locate.

The third and final division of Team Patterns is reserved for special team situations. Here one can note center and other jump set-ups, slow-down tactics, free throw alignments, out-of-bounds plays, fast break situations, and special set plays. Again, the positioning of the other team should be noted whenever possible.

Area II—individual information

Individual Information is the title of the next general

area and it shares the space on the right side of the folder with General Offensive and Defensive Notes. As mentioned earlier, the Individual Information area assumes considerable importance when a team employs a free-lance type of offense. Although the free-lance team's basic formation can be matched-up, individual offensive movements must be noted in order to neutralize the scoring threat. For example, an exceptionally tall and strong team may free-lance from a 2-1-2 set-up. The scouting information should note such important individual information as which players will follow their shots, which are prone to drive and from what direction, who does most of the ball-handling, who are the strongest or weakest scoring threats and what are their favorite shooting areas, and what players are likely to set screens, etc.

Defensive strengths and weaknesses should be spotted by the alert scout and noted very specifically. A wealth of information can be recorded on the individual which will have great bearing on the ultimate defensive and offensive plan. Note this section carefully in the sample report. (See Diagram 60, Part 2, page 201.)

Area III—general offensive and defensive information

This section is the "round-up" portion and is especially designed for information on team tactics that can't be adequately diagramed in the Team Patterns area. Here, remarks on general offense such as the following can be recorded: guards bring the ball down court quickly, team will shoot often before setting up, throw lead pass down court on interception. There are always defensive traits which can be noted: average man-to-man defense (little switching), man-to-man against all out-of-bounds plays,

INDIVIDUAL (AREA II)   GENERAL (AREA III)

NO.	NAME	POS.	HT.	WT.	AGE	YR.
13	SANFORD	G	6-1	170		JR.

LIKES TO FAKE LEFT — DRIVE RIGHT...
GOOD DEFENDER, KEY MAN ON ZONE
PRESS... LUNGES FOR BALL... TWO-
HAND SET... 15-20 FT. JUMPER... BEST
BALL HANDLER... LIKES TO DRIBBLE

32	LEE	F	6-7	205		JR.

HOOKS WELL WITH EITHER HAND...
EXCELLENT REBOUNDER—BIG, AGRES-
SIVE: MUST BE SCREENED OUT... TAKES
HIGH PASS SLIDING ACROSS LANE... 13
FOR 18 FROM FIELD... DEFENSE AVG.

34	THOMAS	C	6-5	200		SR.

STRONGEST MAN... NO CONSCIENCE...
WILL ROUGH YOU UP.. ENJOYS REBOUNDING
—MUST SCREEN OUT ON FREE THROW...
EXCELLENT TAP-IN.. INEFFECTIVE SHOOTER
BEYOND FREE-THROW LINE... GOOD DEF.

25	MARTNELL	F	6-4	195		SR.

PROBABLY BEST SHOOTER... SHORT
JUMPER (10-12 FT.) AND ONE-HANDER
FROM CORNER... MUST BE COVERED
CLOSELY AT ALL TIMES... AVERAGE
DEFENDER

30	SIMPSON	G	6-0	170		SR.

WEAKEST STARTER.. SLUFF ON DEFENSE..
HELPS BRING BALL DOWN COURT... VERY
POOR DEFENSE.. POOR OUTSIDE SHOOTER..
AVG. BALL HANDLER... SLOW GETTING
BACK ON DEF.. CAN BE BEAT ON DRIVE

40	JONES	C	6-3	185		JR.

FAIR SHOOTER... NOT AGGRESSIVE...
POOR DEFENSE

37	GRAY	G	5-9	160		SO.

DID NOT PLAY

27	HOLDER	F	6-0	155		SO.

PLAYED WELL... SET SHOT FROM
CORNER LOOKED GOOD... DRIVES
BASELINE... LIKES TO DRIBBLE...
AVERAGE BALL HANDLER... GOOD
DEFENSE... DOESN'T FAKE EASILY

OFFENSE (MAN-TO-MAN)

1. SPLIT POST WHEN FORWARD
   COVERED.

2. SCREEN OPPOSITE. EFFECTIVE
   BECAUSE OF BIG MAN (32).

3. THEY'LL JAM UP RIGHT SIDE
   OFTEN. 32 DROPS BACK THRU
   LANE ON THIS OPTION FOR EASY
   LAYUP. 13 WORKS THIS WELL:
   HE IS A DECEPTIVE PASSER.

4. AS DIAGRAMMED.

5. (1-3-1 ZONE OFFENSE) FREE
   LANCE.

6. SAME AS ABOVE WITH CUTTERS.
   ZONE OFFENSE LOOKED O.K.
   25 WAS THE ONLY EFFECTIVE
   SHOOTER IN THIS PATTERN.
   WILL TRY TO FEED HIM.

FAST BREAK WHEN THEY HAVE
A CHANCE (FREE LANCE).

* SHOOT CONSTANTLY BEFORE
  SETTING UP.

* EVERYONE LIKES TO DRIVE
  (MUST STOP).

DEFENSE

1. AVERAGE MAN-TO-MAN
   (USED MOSTLY).

2. 1-3-1 ZONE (TRAP IN CORNER
   AND OUT FRONT).

3. ZONE PRESS (AS DIAGRAMMED)
   AFTER MADE FREE THROW
   AND IN LAST 3 MINUTES OF
   BOTH HALVES.

USED 2-1-2 ZONE ABOUT 2
MINUTES EARLY IN GAME.

BIG MEN SCREEN OUT WELL
ON DEFENSE — WILL HAVE TO
TAP-OUT TO REBOUND WITH
THEM.

ZONE AGAINST ALL OUT-OF-
BOUNDS PLAYS.

DEFENSE HAS A TENDENCY TO
TAKE IT SLOWER WHEN THEY
GET 6-10 POINTS AHEAD.

front men on 2-1-2 zone like to put pressure on ball, man-to-man full court press, and so on.

Shot charts

Invariably, coaches will rely on shot charts of the op-position as an integral part of their scouting activities. While this practice can be extremely meaningful, it can also be harmful. The chief problem in the use of shot charts in scouting is the failure on the part of some coaches to "read" the charts correctly. By "reading" charts cor-rectly, we mean that a chart must be considered with cer-tain factors in mind—what type of defense was used, were the close-in shots driving lay-ups or rebounds, what kind of offensive pattern was predominantly employed, etc.

The point to be made here is that while shot charts can provide valuable information, they must be accompanied by an adequate body of information on individual and team strategy—the kind of information supplied by the main report.

Although a chart seems to indicate a potent shooter (Diagram 61), this might not be the case. In this instance, the big man underneath was being double-teamed, allow-ing some easy lay-up shots by the forward sliding across.

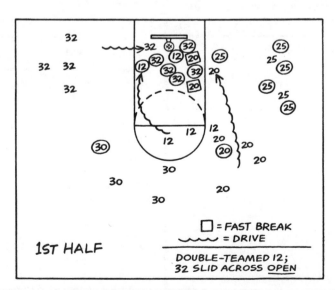

Diagram 61

The main points of analysis in observing shot charts are usually the following:

1. Most prolific shooters
2. Favorite shooting areas of individuals and team patterns
3. Scoring effectiveness outside and in close
4. Most accurate shooters

Personally, if our charts and main report reveal poor shooters, we play the percentages. That is, we plan our defensive strategy so that the poor shooter is allowed a margin of freedom, thus enabling more concentration on the stronger shooters.

A careful study of the sample main report (Diagram 60, Parts 1 and 2) will give a complete understanding of the function of our particular method. The fact that the report is kept directly on a sturdy manila folder dictates a simple system of filing; shot charts of the team may be placed inside, and the whole works is easily accessible whenever the need arises. Simple but thorough, the system outlined in this chapter offers all the essential information needed for planning the most effective offensive and defensive strategy needed to beat the opposition.

The scouting report should be discussed by the coaching staff, at which time the strategy to be employed should be decided upon. The material should be compiled in a simple form and a mimeographed copy given to each player. Every player should have a folder to keep a copy of all scouting reports. At the end of the season this folder should be returned to the coach and destroyed.

Personally, I do not believe a team can be over-scouted. Psychologically, a team should be able to adjust if the opponent does something other than that indicated by the scouting report. Familiarity breeds confidence but a team should be conditioned to the fact that changes are imminent and adjustment to new situations will come about at all times. Over-emphasizing the abilities of the opponent is not desirable but this can be overcome by encouraging the team to help with scouting whenever possible. The scouting report and a change of theory on the part of the opponent is a conditioning situation that should be developed. When presenting the scouting report it is necessary to reiterate the fact that preparation is being made for the effects that were recorded. The opponent may come up with some new theory which will require adjustment during the game, but that is why time-outs are made available.

MATCH-UP SCOUTING SUMMARY

It might be worthwhile at this point, in the way of a summary, to list the special information a scout must consider in his report in order to insure efficient use of the Match-Up.

1. Note the offensive formations. (Even though this may sound simple it is imperative, for the Match-Up will take the same formation as the offense.

2. Record carefully the movements and options of the various offensive formation. (Scoring options must be noted in order to employ the Match-Up's various neutralizing tactics: converging, closing the gap, trapping, etc.).

3. Note the special situations (jump ball, out-of-bounds plays, set plays) so that these maneuvers can be "matched up" in practice sessions.

4. Check individual strengths and weaknesses. (When a team resorts to free-lance tactics, the Match-Up must be ready to take advantage of the individual weak links and to concentrate on the stronger players with over-play.)

5. Get an overall picture of the offensive "style" of

the opponent so that your players are alerted to team and individual habits of the opposition. (An opponent, for example, that plays the breaking game demands the attention of certain key personnel, defensively).

These five points are ones which are of immediate importance in scouting for the Match-Up. Naturally, there are other very meaningful areas of the report. Noting the opposition's defensive strategy in order to capitalize on your own offense is of obvious magnitude. However, this and other points are mentioned in the chapter and need little reiteration.

CHARTING

Almost every coach realizes the need for a device which will check his strategy, point out team and individual strengths and weaknesses, and provide a clue to possible lines of adjustment, offensively and defensively. The mental notes of a coach might serve as this device, but there is always that "margin of human error." Often, one fails to mentally record incidents during the excitement of the game. The answer, of course, is a good system of charting—one that gives information that can be of use at half time, during subsequent practices, and even weeks later as a means of providing a progress report on individuals and the team as a whole. Charting takes the guesswork out of coaching.

Whether you decide to chart many categories or few, it is important to make each one functional for your specific purposes. Later in the explanation of our method, you will note that we keep detailed charts on eleven individual performance items, six team items, as well as complete shot charts on our team and the opposition.

Charting can and should be something more than just

a device enabling players and coaches to find out what's wrong with what they're doing. It can be an effective promotional and motivating artifice which may improve interest and attendance. High Point College and Oglethorpe University have taken advantage of this idea. During the 1962-63 season, these two schools charted both teams during their home games and, at half time, released to the spectators mimeographed resumes of the charts which the coaches carried to their dressing rooms. The element of "audience participation," so vital to maximum enjoyment of any recreational activity, was introduced and resulted in a new enthusiasm and interest on the part of the spectators.

The value of audience participation is something that should be considered by every coach. This can readily be seen at Dillard High School of Fort Lauderdale, Florida. Here, the spectators take part in the game by responding verbally and in unison to certain types of play on the court. For example, when a jump rebound, as opposed to a passive rebound, is made by a Dillard player, the crowd responds with a loud "CLEAN" for clean rebound. This type of spectator activity has had positive results for the Dillard players in that rebounding has assumed virtually the same "prestige" as scoring. Whether you chart like Oglethorpe and High Point or chant like Dillard High School—audience participation promises more interest and bigger gates.

A method of charting

Once again, there are many methods of charting. It's up to the individual coach to devise his own—taking the best aspects of charting he can find and putting together a system which is perfect for his purposes. Our method was compiled over long years of trial and error, careful

Basketball Statistics Chart

PER. FOULS	NAME	REBOUND OFF.	REBOUND DEF.	REBOUND TOT.	B.P.	TRAV.	HELD BALL	FUM.	VIOL.	TOT.	GAIN BALL	ASSIST	BLOCK SHOT
IIII	SMITH (23)	卌 IIII	卌 卌	7 / 12		I		II	II	4 / 1	III		II
卌	WIEDEMAN (31)	I	卌 III	4 / 5			II	II		4 / 0	II	II	
IIII	STANDART (53)	卌 II	卌 II	6 / 8						0 / 0	IIII	卌	
I	GRAU (33)	I	I	1 / 1	II					1 /	I	卌 I	
I	BOYD (15)			0 / 0	I					0 / 1		IIII	
I	SIMS (43)		I	0 / 1						0 / 0			
	PARSONS (21)		II	0 / 2						0 / 0			
	McDERMOTT (25)			0 / 0						0 / 0			
	VOIGHT (13)			0 / 0						0 / 0			
I	DOWNEY (11)			0 / 0						0 / 0			
	WILLIAMS (35)			0 / 0						0 / 0			
	DAVIS (51)			0 / 0						0 / 0			
HALF TOTALS 1ST / 2ND		8 / 10	10 / 19	18 / 29	3 / 0	1 / 0	0 / 2	3 / 1	2 / 0	9 / 3	4 / 6	9 / 8	1 / 3
GAME TOTALS		18	29	47	3	1	2	4	2	12	10	17	4

SCORING ATTEMPT

Category	Attempt 1	Attempt 2
MAN-MAN (WEAVE)	3-5	
ZONE (1-3-1)	1-7	
ZONE (FLA.)	5-15	
FAST BRK.	5-7	8-13
OUT OF BOUNDS	2-4	0-3
REBOUND	4-12	2-8
FREE LANCE	1-2	2-4
JUMP BALL	1-1	1-2
PRESS	1-3	2-5
FOUL	0-3	2-4

Diagram 62

scrutiny of many other systems—finally resulting in what will be explained on the following pages. For ease of understanding we will divide our particular method into four general headings: Charting Personnel, Uses, Categories, and Shot Charts. A sample of our main chart (Diagram 62) will be of principal significance.

Charting personnel

Our game charting duties are shared by three people. The job of keeping the main chart is usually delegated to the assistant coach. As this duty requires some practice to perform with efficiency it is best to have the same person keep the chart throughout the season.

One person, usually a manager, is assigned to keep a shot chart on our own team while another manager, or faculty members, keep a shot chart on the opposition.

All three personnel make hasty half time compilations of their charts (adequate space allotted for this in all charts) for use at intermissions.

Accuracy and pride are the watchwords which should be instilled by the coach in his chart men. They must understand that they are vital to victory.

Uses

One of the most important uses of charting is the obvious half time analysis. A preponderance of "marks" in one of the major areas will usually provide the key which a coach needs to readjust his strategy, personnel, or both, for the next half of play.

A glance at the total number of mistakes (losses of ball) during the half time can often indicate where a team might be having problems.

In order to make maximum use of the charts at half

time it is imperative that the time period be considered adequately. Although this period will vary between colleges and high schools, a rough estimation can be noted which will serve both needs rather well. Allow the boys about three minutes, after entering the dressing room, to get a drink, use the bathroom, and make other necessary adjustments. The coach uses this time to study the shot chart of his team and the opponent's along with the individual and team performances recorded on the main chart. The next five to ten minutes should be spent in making the necessary adjustments or corrections based on the facts which the charts reveal. The remaining time should be spent in warm-up for the second half.

We firmly believe that the half time priority be given to the purposes which your charts have been designed to meet. A team that needs to take the full period making adjustments in the dressing room should not feel it is depriving itself of warm-up time.

Long-range uses of charting are in the hands of the head coach. He may choose to hand out, from time to time, a summary of individual performances based on the charts. Here, pride in individual statistics such as rebounding, assists, stolen balls, and blocked shots can be exploited. There is always the latent competition between players on the same team that can be brought out to the team's advantage by naming the leaders in these various categories.

The coach may also use the charts intensively as a guideline to the types of drills (fundamental or other) which will be necessary to include in ensuing practice sessions. He may, in studying shot charts, uncover personnel who have proven ineffective scorers from certain areas —thus enabling specific shooting drills to be introduced for players who need them.

Regardless of how a coach uses his charts, he should study them carefully and file them later in some organized manner.

Major categories

A cursory glance at the sample main chart (Diagram 62) will show that our system divides the important charting items into three major areas: Rebounds (which also includes the category at the right)—Gain Ball, Loss of Ball, and Scoring Attempts. The first two areas are concerned with the individual player while the latter is a team statistic.

One of the first things we consider at the half is rebounding—if we aren't getting our share, we try to figure out why. The rebounding heading is divided into offensive and defensive. With the chart's unique cross-totalizing capability, it is easy to calculate and indicate half time totals for both the team and individual. Just as vital to this general area is the Gain Ball column. This category reveals the number of stolen balls, interceptions, or loose balls we have managed to acquire. A gained ball of this variety is just as valuable and deserves just as much recognition as a jump rebound.

All the individual statistics are recorded with a simple vertical pencil mark.

The second major category, and often the most important one in close games, is the Loss of Ball category. Another look at Diagram 62 shows this area divided into five sub-categories. In order, they are as follows: bad passes, traveling, held ball, fumbles, and violations. Each is self-explanatory with the exception, perhaps, of held ball and violations. We consider a held ball one in which we are guilty of being tied up for a jump situation. Violations is a miscellaneous column which is for any other mishap (three-second violation, offensive charging, back court, palming, etc.) which results in our team losing possession of the ball. We feel it is necessary for analyzing purposes to name only the categories which are most frequently violated and which, for one reason or other, give our teams the biggest problems.

The third major category—one that probably makes our system unique in some respects—is the team statistical area, Scoring Attempts. This category was included in our main chart largely on the advice of Florida State's J. K. (Bud) Kennedy, who was one of the first to use it with success.

In the Scoring Attempts category we can really take the guess work out of offensive adjustment. Here, we can easily see how effective our various offensive attacks have been.

If we take a shot from a particular offensive maneuver and do not score we simply make a vertical mark. If we score, we encircle this mark. Although we divide our Scoring Attempts category into nine sub-categories, this will not always be a suitable delineation. The basic man-to-man and zone categories can be subdivided into specific variations.

A look at this section of the sample chart at half time shows that our zone attack, particularly our "Florida" offense, has been going just below average. Although we have made a few fast break attempts, we have been highly successful. This information, coupled with the knowledge that our rebounding has been strong, would indicate a definite line of strategy for the next half.

As you can see we chart our out-of-bounds, rebound, jump ball, and free-lance offensive attempts. We even chart special situations like scoring from plays which are set up when the other team is shooting a foul shot, or scoring from our full court offenses against zone or man-to-man presses and traps.

The minor categories not mentioned thus far are Personal Fouls, Blocked Shots, and Assists. Each of these we find highly functional, especially the Blocked Shot column which fits in nicely with the Match-Up theory.

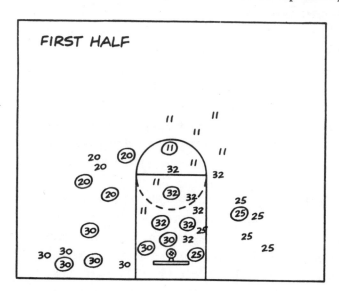

Diagram 63

NO.	NAME	FGA	FGM	PCT.
30	DAVIS	8	5	.625
20	SMITH	5	3	.600
32	JONES	8	3	.375
25	GRAY	7	2	.286
11	GREEN	8	1	.125
	TOTALS	36	14	.389

NO.	NAME	FTA	FTM	PCT.
30	DAVIS	3	2	.667
20	SMITH	2	1	.500
32	JONES	2	0	.000
25	GRAY	4	3	.750
11	GREEN	3	2	.667
	TOTALS	14	8	.571

FREE THROWS: (30) 30, (30), 11, (25)(25), (20) 20, (11)(11), 32 32, 25 (25)

Shot charts

The shot charts kept during the game, our team's and the opposition's, are comprehensive. See the sample chart in Diagram 63. We not only note the shots taken from the field but are careful to keep a running account of free throw proficiency, as well.

Not *keeping* the chart, but *reading* the chart correctly is the coach's distinct duty. As was pointed out in the section on the scouting report, you should be able to determine from your team's shot chart and the opposition's, who is taking the most shots and who is hitting with the greatest degree of accuracy, what areas of the floor are the most vulnerable or seem to be "favorite" shooting areas, who are the players who are less of a threat than others from the field or from the free throw line. These are some of the things which must be read into shot charts by the coach.

In conclusion, then, one cannot fail to underestimate the value of a complete and functional system of both charting and scouting. We have found the key to efficiency in these departments to be simplicity and organization. First, devise a method that is simple, one that gives a maximum amount of the "right" kind of information without causing the scout or chart man to lose contact with the activity that is going on in front of him. Second, make sure that you organize and file every scouting report and chart so that, when the need arises, the information is at hand.

Index

A

Aids Associates of Pompano
  Beach, 41

B

Back-line adjustments, 86–87, 92
Bad passes, forcing of, 62
Base-line defense, 27, 72, 82–85
  95, 106, 119–126, 137, 139
Basic rules, 78–101
  (*See also* Positions)
Big pivot man, 19, 23–24
"Blind pick" from weave, 112
Blocked shot, 100–101
Blocking-out, 32–33, 138
  drills for, 72–77
  from front line, 72
  from inside, 157
  on strong side, 72
  on weak side, 72
Boxer's stance, 42

C

Center-forward screen and
  roll, 116–118
Center jump, fast break
  from, 173–178
Changeover drill, 143
Changeover from offense to
  defense, 140–143

Charting, 72, 100, 182, 205–213
  categories in, 210–212
  personnel assigned to, 208
  shot charts, 196, 202–204, 213
  uses of, 208–210
Cheap baskets, 142–143
Circle drill, 98
Close-the-gap drill, 68–70
Code for jump ball defense,
  144–145, 148
Coker, Larry, 163
Combination defenses, 16,
  18, 21, 27, 34–35
Continuity offenses, 15–18, 104,
  111, 121–125, 127–131
Converging, 23–24, 25, 34,
  70–71, 84–85, 94–96, 112, 139
Court size, Match-Up and, 35–37
Cover-Jump play, 148–150
Cross court pass, 109
Cutters, 17, 19, 28–29, 83, 91
  defensing of, 87, 107–111
  overplaying of 84, 87, 90–92,
  95, 109, 110, 117, 118

D

Daytona Beach High School,
  30–31
Deceptive passes, 23, 25, 97, 126
Defense (s) (*See also*
  Match-Up defense)

Defense (s) (*cont.*)
  changeover from offense
     to, 140–143
  combination, 16, 18, 21, 27,
     34–35
  individual, development
     of, 18–19
  patterned, 17, 21
  press, 103–104
Defensive average, 16
Defensive stance, drills for
     41–49
Dillard High School, 206
Direct pass to pivot man,
     stopping of, 24
Double cut through, 108–109
Double screen, 26
Double teaming, 23–25, 62, 84–85,
     105, 106, 118, 126, 152, 183
Down court defense, 140–143
Downward slap, 45
Dribble, defensing of, 24–25
Dribble Get-Back-On-Defense
     drill, 57–59
Drills, 38–77
  changeover, 143
  circle, 98
  for defensive stance, 41–49
  dummy, 166, 192
  fast break (*see* Fast break)
  footwork (*see* Footwork and
     shifting drills)
  "keep away," 97–98
  lead pass, 172
  one-on-one, 140
  Pepper The Post, 97
  peripheral vision, 96–98
  Position Master, use of,
     in, 40–41
  three-on-two, 140
  two-on-one, 140
  two-on-two, 140
  weave, 111–112
Dummy drills, 166, 192

E

Eye defects, drills for
     improvement of, 96–98

F

Fake plays, 48, 49, 107, 142
Fast break, 22, 28, 31, 33–34,
     94, 140, 152, 158–193
  from center jump, 173–178
  drills for, 166, 169, 172,
     187–193
     Follow-The-Lay-Up, 189–191
     Tap-Out Lay-Up, 187–188
     Tap-Out, Pass-Out, 169, 172,
       192–193
     three-line, 189, 191
  from foul shot, 152
  free throw, 182–187
  jump formations, 181–182
  lanes, 34, 164–166
  from man-to-man
     defense, 34
  pass-out, 168–169, 171–172
  personnel and position
     requirements, 94–95,
       161–164
  quick second tap, 178–180
  from rebound, 33–34, 159, 168
  from tap-out, 94, 168–171
  three-lane, 164–167
  trailers, 34, 95–96, 142–143,
     160–164, 166–167
Feints, 49, 142
Figure eight continuity
     weave, 111
Five man weave, 111
Florida Class AA State
     Tournament, 134–135
Florida State High School
     Tournament, 30–31
Florida State University, 97, 211
Follow-the-lay-up drill,
     189–191
Foot handicaps, 43

Footwork and shifting
drills, 41–77
blocking-out, 72–77
Close-The-Gap, 68–70
converging, 70–71
directional slide and
shift, 50–52
Dribble Get-Back-On-Defense,
57–59
One-Two-Three, 59–61
rebounding, 72–77
Rubber Ball, 55–57
shift-slide-pass, 54–55
Short-Cut, 63–64
start and stop, 52–54
Three-On-One
Full-Court, 61–63
without limitations,
62, 67–68
With a Screen, 62, 65–67, 112
Forward pivot, 73–74, 175
Foul shot
fast break from, 152
made, outlet pass on, 183–185
missed, tap-out, on 153,
156, 157, 182–183, 185–186
Foul trouble, advantage of
Match-Up in, 30–31
Free lance offense, 34, 105, 119,
144, 159–160, 200
Free throw, defensing of,
151–156 (*See also* Foul shot)
Free throw circle, tap to, 169–170
Free throw fast break, 182–187
Free throw shooter, 153–154
Front line
adjustments in, 86–87, 92
block-out from, 72
long rebound from, 74
swinging of, 91–93, 108,
109, 121
Full-court offense, 58, 61–62
Full-court pass, 152
Full-court press, 58, 71
Full-court Three-On-One
drill, 61–63

Full-court trap, 153
Fuson, Shelvie, 29

G

Guard-forward screen and
roll, 116–118

H

Hale, Bruse, 61
Half-court defense, 143, 152
Half-court three line attack, 191
Half-court trap, 152, 153
Half-court weave (*see* Weave)
Hall High School, 27
Hand position, importance
of, 45–46
Hand signals, 57, 60–61, 136
Handicaps
foot, 43
sight, drills for, 96–98
Harassment, 22, 26, 189, 190
Henderson, Cam, 50
High Point College, 206
Hillsborough High School,
134–135
Hundley, Rod, 189
Hurried passes, 25, 141
Hurried shots, 141, 142

I

Intercepting
of passes, 25, 62, 115, 160, 182
of tap-out, 170–171

J

"Jam" areas, zone, 138–139
Jump ball defense, 35, 143–146,
159, 160
Jump formations, 146–148
fast break, 181–182
Jump shot, 24, 117, 129, 141–142

K

"Keep away" drills, 97–98
Kennedy, J. K. "Bud," 97, 211
Kentucky, University of, 27–28

L

Lanes, fast break, 34, 164–166
Lay-up 40–41, 141–142, 165–167,
    176, 187–191
Lead pass, 84, 86, 108, 117, 119,
    177, 184, 187, 193
  drills for, 172
Lenoir Rhyne College, 30
Long tap, 175–178
Loose ball, 34, 71, 74, 97, 159–160
Low post, 126–127

M

Man-to-man defense, 15–22,
    28–29, 32–37, 81
  acquiring lanes from, 34
  corner position, strong side,
    82–83, 87
  fast break from, 34
    (See also Fast break)
  front position, weak side, 85
  middle position, 85–86
  swinging the front line, 91–93
Marshall University, 50, 169
Match-Up defense, 14–37,
    102–158
  advantages of, 22–37
    big slow men, effective
      against, 29–30
    driving, screening offense,
      effective against, 26–27
    in fast break, 33–34 (See
      also Fast break)
    in foul trouble, 30–31
    outside shooter,
      troublesome to, 27–29
    in rebounding, 32–33
      (See also Rebounding)
  base-line, 27, 72, 82–85, 95,
    106, 119–126, 137, 139

Match-Up defense (cont.)
  basic rules for, 78–101,
    (See also Positions)
  blocking-out
    (see Blocking-out)
  continuity offenses, 15–18,
    104, 111, 121–125, 127–131
  converging, 23–24, 25, 34,
    70–71, 84–85, 94–96,
    112, 139
  court size and, 35–37
  Cover Jump play, 148–150
  cutters (see Cutters)
  double teaming, 23–25, 62,
    84–85, 105, 106, 118, 126,
    152, 183
  down court, 140–143
  dribble, 24–25
  drills for (see Drills)
  fast break from (see Fast
    break)
  free throw, 151–156
  half-court, 143, 152
  jump ball, 35, 143–146, 159,
    160
  jump formations, 146–148
  low post, 126–127
  man-to-man (see Man-to-man
    defense)
  new defensive fronts
    formed in, 19–21
  one-on-one situation, 26,
    118, 177
  one-three-one jump, 150–151
  one-three-one offensive
    formations, 28, 68, 79–80,
    84, 118–126
  out-of-bounds play, 35, 133–
    140
  overload, 19, 28–29, 105–107
  personnel requirements (see
    Personnel requirements)
  pick-off play, 170–172
  positions (see Positions)
  screen, 17, 19, 26–29, 112,
    166–167

Match-Up defense *(cont.)*
  screen *(cont.)*
    from weak side, 139–140
  screen and roll play, 21,
    94, 115–118
  shooter, covering of, 24,
    156–157
  sluffing, 28, 32, 74–77, 83–84,
    91–93, 107, 110–115,
    117–120, 123–126, 129,
    131, 141
  strong points of all defenses
    combined in, 18–19
  tandem, 34, 140–141, 152–154
  three-on-one situation, 142
  trapping, 71, 94, 96, 103–104,
    109, 128
  two-on-one situation, 142
  two-three formation, 68–71,
    79–81, 90, 137–138
  weave *(see* Weave)
  zone *(see* Zone defense)
  zone "jam" areas, 138–139
Mental approach, importance
  of, 47–48
Miami, University of, 61
Miami High School, 134–135
Middlesboro High School, 28–29
Missed foul shot, tap-out on,
  153, 156, 157, 182–183,
  185–186
Moving screen, 26
Multiple offense, 103

N

N.A.I.B. Tournament, 169
Newberry College, 99, 187, 189

O

Off-center tap-out, 171
Offense(s)
  changeover to defense from,
    140–143
  continuity, 15–18, 104, 111,
    121–125, 127–131

Offense (s) *(cont.)*
  defensing of *(see* Match-Up
    defense)
  free lance, 34, 105, 119, 144,
    159–160, 200
  full-court, 58, 61–62
  multiple, 103
  one-three-one formation, 28,
    68, 79–80, 84, 118–126
  potency of, reasons for, 15
  three-two formation, 68,
    79–80, 90, 111
Offensive wing men, spreading
  of, 118
Oglethorpe Invitational
  Tournament, 99
Oglethorpe University, 206
One-handed jump, 168–169
One-on-one drill, 140
One-three-one defensive jump,
  150–151
One-two-three drill, 59–61
Open set shot, 129
Option plays, 104, 124, 136,
  138–139, 166
Out-of-bounds play, defensing
  of, 35, 133–140
Outlet pass, 34, 140, 152, 154,
  159, 160, 162, 182, 183,
  187, 193
  interception of, 182
  on made foul shot, 183–185
  stealing of, 153
Outside shooter, 89, 91, 123–124
  Match-Up troublesome to,
    27–29
Overload, defensing of, 19, 28–29,
  105–107
Overplaying of cutters, 84, 87,
  90–92, 95, 109, 110, 117, 118

P

Pass-out, fast break, 168–169,
  171–172

Pass-out, fast break (*cont.*)
  bad, forcing of, 62
  cross court, 109
  deceptive, 23, 25, 97, 126
  direct, to pivot man, stopping
      of, 24
  full-court, 152
  hurried, 25, 141
  intercepting of, 25, 62, 115,
      160, 182
  lead, 84, 86, 108, 117, 119,
      177, 184, 187, 193
    drills for, 172
  outlet (*see* Outlet pass)
  release, 162, 169, 177, 183
  stealing of, 25, 110, 153, 159
Patterned defenses, 17, 21
Pepper the post drill, 97
Peripheral vision, drills for,
    96–98
Personnel requirements
  for fast break, 94–95, 161–164
  left-corner, 95, 163–164
  left-front, 94
  middle position, 95–96, 164
  for rebounding, 95
  right-corner, 95, 164
  right-front, 94, 162
  trailers, 95–96
Pick-off play, defense against,
    170–172
Pivot
  forward, 73–74, 175
  reverse, 72–73, 177
Pivot man, big, 19, 23–24
Pompano Beach, Aids
    Associates of, 41
Pompano Beach Senior High
    School, 39, 163, 175
Position Master, use of, 40–41
Positions, 78–101
  back-line adjustments, 86–87
  corner
    converge in, 71
    left-, 79

Positions (*cont.*)
  corner (*cont.*)
    left- (*cont.*)
      personnel requirements
          for, 95, 163–164
      middle position to, 87–91
    right-, 79
      personnel requirements
          for, 95, 164
    screen and roll attacked
        from, 115
    strong side, 82–83, 87–89
    weak side, 83–84, 88
  front
    converge in, 71
    left-, 79
      personnel requirements
          for, 94
    right-, 79
      personnel requirements
          for, 94, 162
    screen and roll attacked
        from, 115–118
    strong side, 84–85, 89
    weak side, 85, 88
  middle, 79, 85–86
    converge in, 71
    to the corner, 87–91
    personnel requirements
        for, 95–96, 164
Press
  full-court, 58, 71
  trap, 153
Press defense, 103–104

Q

Quick second tap, 178–180

R

Rebounding, 22, 30, 32–33,
    154–156
  drills for, 72–77
  fast break and, 33–34, 159,
      168 (*See also* Fast break)
  from front position, weak
      side, 85

Rebounding (*cont.*)
  from middle position, 87–89
  personnel requirements
    for, 95
Release pass, 162, 169, 177, 183
Reverse pivot, 72–73, 177
Roamer, 84, 119–121
Rubber ball drill, 55–57
"Run and shoot" game, 27

S

Safety man, 34, 95, 175, 177, 180
Sagging, 23–24
Scouting, 19, 47, 156, 194–196
Scouting reports, 31–32, 84, 86,
    87, 108, 120, 141, 153, 173,
    196–205
  areas covered on, 198–204
    general offensive and
      defensive information,
      200–204
    individual information,
      199–200
    team patterns, 198–199
Screen, 17, 19, 26–29, 94,
    112, 166–167
  from weak side, defense
    against, 139–140
Screen drill, three-on-one
    with, 62, 65–67, 112
Screen and roll play, 21, 94,
    115–118
Senses, use of, 96–100
Set screen, 26
Shifting, drills for (*see*
    Footwork and shifting drills)
Shooter
  covering of, 24, 156–157
  free throw, 153–154
  outside, 89, 91, 123–124
    Match-Up troublesome to,
      27–29
Short-cut drill, 63–64
Shot charts, 196, 202–204, 213
Sight handicaps, drills for, 96–98

Signals
  hand, 57, 60–61, 136
  verbal, 112, 136, 144–145, 166
  whistle, 57
Slap, downward, 45
Sluffing, 28, 32, 74–77, 83–84,
    91–93, 107, 110–115,
    117–120, 123–126, 129,
    131, 141
Soft tap, 147, 180
Spreading of offensive wing
    men, 118
Stance, defensive, drills for
    41–49
Stealing
  of passes, 25, 110, 153, 159
  of tap, 169
Stetson University, 73
Strong side, 81
  blocking-out on, 72
  corner position, 82–83, 87–89
  front position, 84–85, 89
Swinging of front line, 91–93,
    108, 109, 121
Switching on weave, 111–114

T

Talk, importance of 65, 98–99,
    129, 143
Tandem defense, 34, 140–141,
    152–154
Tap, 146–151
  control of, 173–180
  to free throw circle, 169–170
  long, 175–178
  quick second, 178–180
  soft, 147, 180
  stealing of, 169
Tap-out, 94, 168–171
  intercepting of, 170–171
  on missed foul shot, 153, 156,
    157, 182–183, 185–186
  off-center, 171
Tap-out lay-up drill, 187–188

Tap-out, pass-out drill, 169,
    172, 192–193
Three-lane fast break, 164–167
Three-line drills, 189, 191
Three man weave, 111
Three-on-one drills
    full-court, 61–63
    without limitations, 62, 67–68
    with a screen, 62, 65–67, 112
Three-on-two drill, 140
Three-quarter court trap, 153
Throw-in player, 183
Trailers, 34, 95–96, 142–143,
    160–164, 166–167
Trap
    full-court, 153
    half-court, 152, 153
    three-quarter court, 153
Trap press, 153
Trapping, 71, 94, 96, 103–104,
    109, 128
    of weave, 25–26, 114–115
Turnover play, 153
Two-man zone defense, 141–142
Two-on-one drill, 140
Two-on-two drill, 140

U

Uneven theory, zone defense, 68
Unison movement, zone defense,
    137

V

Verbal signals, 112, 136,
    144–145, 166

Vision, peripheral, drills for
    96–98

W

Weak side, 81
    blocking-out on, 72
    corner position, 83–84, 88
    front position, 85, 88
    overplay on, 111
    screen from, defense against,
        139–140
Weave
    "blind pick" from, 112
    figure eight continuity, 111
    five man, 111
    switching on, 111–114
    three man, 111
    trapping of, 25–26, 114–115
Wells, Billy, 30
West Virginia University, 189
Whistle signals, 57
Wilkes, Glenn, 73
Wing men, offensive, spreading
    of, 118

Z

Zone "jam" areas, 138–139
Zone defense, 15–21, 27–29,
    34–37, 68, 81
    front position, weak side, 85
    out-of-bounds play, 137–139
    two-three, 69–70, 137–138
    two-man, 141–142
    uneven theory, 68
    unison movement, 137
Zone "jam" areas, 138–139